The Pocket

IRISH PUB

COOKBOOK

Gill Books
Hume Avenue, Park West, Dublin 12

www.gillbooks.ie

Gill Books is an imprint of M.H. Gill & Co.

Copyright © Teapot Press Ltd 2016

ISBN: 978-0-7171-6920-7

This book was created and produced by Teapot Press Ltd

Recipes compiled by Fiona Biggs
Designed by Tony Potter
Picture research and photography by Ben Potter
Home economics by Imogen Tyler
Edited by Ruth Mahony

Printed in EU

This book is typeset in Garamond and Dax

A CIP catalogue record for this book is available
from the British Library.

5 4 3 2

THE POCKET
IRISH
PUB
COOKBOOK

Fiona Biggs

A lovely day for a
GUINNESS

Gill Books

Contents

8   **Introduction**

Soups, Starters & Bar Snacks

12   Parsnip & Apple Soup
14   Potato & Black Pepper Soup
16   Leek & Potato Soup
18   Simple Onion Soup
20   Roasted Red Pepper & Sun-dried Tomato soup
22   Pea & Ham Soup
24   Creamy Courgette Soup
26   Potato & Vegetable Soup
28   *The Galway Oyster Festival*
30   Smoked Haddock & Mushroom Chowder
32   Galway Oyster Bisque
34   Dublin Bay Prawns
36   Smoked Mackerel Pâté
38   Prawn Cocktail
40   Smoked Haddock Fishcakes
42   Scallops Wrapped in Bacon
44   Festival Oysters
46   Golden Scampi
48   Stuffed Mussels
50   Seafood Platter
52   Smoked Fish Platter
54   Italian Antipasti Platter
56   Irish Cheese Platter
58   Vegetable Platter with Aïoli
60   Smoked Bacon & Potato Cake
62   Chicken Liver Pâté
64   Black Pudding with Fried Apple Rings
66   Deep-fried Irish Camembert with Redcurrant Sauce
68   Roast Pork, Chutney & Pickle Onion Open Sandwich
70   Prawn & Avocado Open Sandwich
72   Smoked Salmon, Cream Cheese & Cucumber Open Sandwich
74   Beetroot, Goat's Cheese and Baby Spinach Open Sandwic

Main Dishes

78 Dublin Coddle
80 Irish Stew
82 Sweet & Spicy Beef
84 *The Guinness Harp*
86 Zesty Beef & Guinness Casserole
88 Steak & Stout Pie
90 Baked Limerick Ham with Parsley Sauce
92 Roast Wicklow Lamb
94 Quiche Lorraine
96 Caramelised Cherry Tomato & Goat's Cheese Tart
98 Roasted Red Pepper & Feta Tart
100 Wild Mushroom Risotto
102 Lamb Hotpot
104 Roast Pork Loin with Crackling
106 Pork Fillet Stuffed with Prunes
108 Lemon Parmigiana Chicken Rissoles
110 Turkey & Ham Rissoles with Zesty Cranberry Sauce
112 Creamy Chicken Pie
114 Shepherd's Pie
116 Caramelised Red Onion & Baby Spinach Tart
118 Sherried Lamb's Kidneys on Fried Sourdough Bread
120 Stuffed Salmon en Croûte
122 Smoked Salmon Tart
124 Dublin Lawyer
126 Trout with Herb Butter
128 Luxury Fish Pie
130 Seafood Mornay
132 Monkfish Wrapped in Parma Ham

Sides & Salads

136 Chicken Salad
138 Warm Bacon Salad with Pine Nuts

140 Baby Spinach Salad with Blue Cheese & Walnut Dressing
142 Classic Green Salad
144 *A Tale of Irish Cheesemaking*
146 Mixed Salad
148 Colcannon
150 Boxty
152 New Potato Salad with Mint
154 Crunchy Fried Potatoes
156 Roast Potatoes
158 Cheesy Potatoes with Garlic & Cream
160 Jacket Potatoes (and Toppings)
162 Minted Peas
164 Baby Carrots with Dill
166 Creamed Spinach
168 Spiced Red Cabbage
170 Kale with Lemon & Butter
172 Creamy Onion Bake
174 Champ
176 Roast Parsnips
178 Baked Leeks

Desserts
182 Pear & Chocolate Tart
184 Chocolate Whiskey Mousse Ta
186 Irish Cream Cheesecake
188 Blueberry Cheesecake
190 Raspberry & Chocolate Roula
192 Lemon Tart
194 Apple Charlotte
196 Apple Pie with Cream
198 Golden Syrup Tart
200 Rhubarb & Ginger Crumble
202 Luxury Bread & Butter Puddir
204 Banoffee Pie
206 Pavlova
208 Brown Bread Ice Cream
210 Carrageen Pudding with Blackberry Coulis
212 Sherry Trifle
214 Tiramisù
216 Sparkling Raspberry Jellies

Bakes & Cakes

220 White Buttermilk Scones
222 Wholemeal Scones
224 Brown Soda Bread
226 Brown Bread
228 White Soda Bread
230 Crunchy Savoury Oatcakes
232 Cheese & Herb Crackers
234 Irish Apple Cake
236 Brack

Drinks

240 Irish Coffee
242 Hot Whiskey
244 *The Story of Irish Whiskey*
246 Hot Port
248 Black Velvet
250 Guinness & Black
252 Black Adder
254 Scailtín

256 **Credits**

Introduction

The pub is a fixture in the Irish social landscape. There are large ones and small ones, most with bars and lounges, some with snugs; some are located in hotels, while others are on the same premises as the general grocery store in some smaller rural communities. The pub is where people go to relax, let their hair down, meet their friends, have some good conversation and enjoy a bit of conviviality. In the past pubs were primarily establishments that sold alcohol, with a limited range of food available – the soup and sandwich lunch was a staple of office workers and people on the move, the soup almost invariably produced from large catering packs of bland-tasting powder and the sandwich made on processed white bread with a processed cheese or ham (or cheese and ham) filling, sometimes toasted in a heatproof cellophane bag. If you were lucky, there might be some roast meat from a carvery served with overcooked, tired-looking vegetables, or chicken in a basket with chips.

How things have changed! Pub-goers have developed discerning palates in tandem with Ireland's rising fortunes and now only good food, properly prepared, will do. At the simple end of the scale, the soup is usually delicious and home-made, served with fresh soda bread or scones and the cheese and ham sandwiches are filled with mature Cheddar cheese and moist baked Limerick ham. Many pubs now offer a huge variety of meals of all kinds, from hearty stews and casseroles such as Irish stew (page 80) and sweet and spicy beef (page 82) to elegant sharing platters, delicious salads, luxurious seafood dishes and savoury tarts. Desserts are an important part of the pub grub experience, ranging from simple apple pie with cream (page 196) to classically elegant lemon tart (page 192) and lusciously creamy tiramisù (page 214). While pub fare is usually based on the best of what Ireland has traditionally produced for the dinner table, it is now enlivened with interesting herbs and unexpected flavours. Ordinary dishes such as potato cakes are enhanced with tasty specks of smoked bacon, while humble black pudding is served with succulent fried apple rings.

Far from being drinking establishments with the possibility of some food, pubs have become culinary destinations in their own right. Food, drink and a fair likelihood of a bit of craic, all under one roof – what more could you ask for?

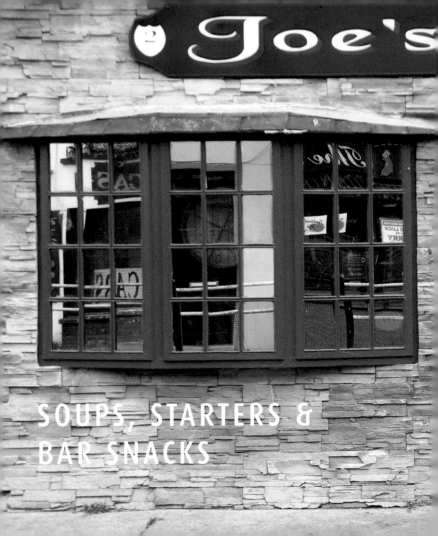

SOUPS, STARTERS &
BAR SNACKS

INGREDIENTS

25 g/1 oz butter
450 g/1 lb parsnips, peeled and sliced
1 Bramley apple, peeled and chopped
1.2 litres/2 pints vegetable stock
½ tsp dried sage
2 cloves
single cream, chopped fresh parsley and fried apple slices, to garnish

Parsnip & Apple Soup

A deliciously creamy yet fresh-tasting soup that combines two ingredients, each with a sweetness of their own.

METHOD

Melt the butter in a large saucepan, then add the parsnips and apple. Cover and cook over a low heat for 10 minutes.

Add the stock, sage and cloves and simmer until the parsnip is softened. Remove and discard the cloves, then pour the content of the pan into a blender and blend until smooth.

Pour the soup into warmed bowls, add a swirl of cream to each then garnish with parsley and fried apple slices and serve immediately.

SERVES 4

INGREDIENTS

2 tbsp sunflower oil
large knob of butter
1 large onion, finely chopped
2 large potatoes, cut into 1-cm/½-inch cubes
500 ml/18 fl oz milk
500 ml/18 fl oz hot vegetable stock
1 tsp whole black peppercorns
pinch of salt
freshly ground black pepper, to garnish

Potato & Black Pepper Soup

This delicious and warming soup is given an unexpected hint of spice with the addition of black peppercorns.

METHOD

Put the oil and butter into a saucepan and heat over a medium heat until the butter is melted. Add the onion, cover the pan and cook for 2–3 minutes until the onion is translucent.

Add the potatoes and cook for a further 5–10 minutes.

Add the milk, stock and peppercorns and bring to a simmer, then reduce the heat and cook for 15–20 minutes until the potatoes are tender. Add the salt.

Transfer the soup to a food processor in batches and process until smooth, making sure that none of the peppercorns remains whole.

Divide the soup among four warmed bowls, garnish with ground pepper and serve immediately.

SERVES 4

INGREDIENTS

1.5 litres/2½ pints
water

10 potatoes, peeled
and sliced

5 leeks, trimmed
and thinly sliced

4–6 tbsp milk

salt and freshly
ground black pepper

2–3 tbsp snipped
fresh chives, to
garnish

Leek & Potato Soup

This soup is delicious on a cold day – a
real winter warmer.

METHOD

Put the potatoes and leeks into a large saucepan of salted wate
bring to the boil and cook for 15–20 minutes, or until tender.

Remove from the heat and mash the vegetables in the liquid.
Add salt and pepper to taste and return to the heat. Stir in the
milk and heat until hot, but not boiling.

Serve in warmed bowls, garnished with chives.

SERVES 6–8

INGREDIENTS

2 tbsp olive oil
2 onions, chopped
2 tbsp plain flour
1.2 litres/2 pints
vegetable stock
3 potatoes, diced
crusty bread or rolls
and butter, to serve

Simple Onion Soup

Onion soup is best served with crusty bread or rolls and lots of butter.

METHOD

Heat the oil in a large saucepan, add the onions and fry until softened. Add the flour and stock and mix to combine.

Add the potatoes and cook over a low heat for 30 minutes, or until the potatoes have broken down.

Serve in warmed bowls with bread and butter.

SERVES 4

INGREDIENTS

3 red peppers, halved and deseeded

1 onion, unpeeled and halved

4 garlic cloves, unpeeled

2 tbsp olive oil

25 g/1 oz butter

2 celery sticks, roughly chopped

450 ml/16 fl oz vegetable stock

3 tbsp sun-dried tomato purée

1 tsp dried chilli flakes

500 g/1 lb 2 oz canned chopped tomatoes

salt and freshly ground black pepper

fresh rosemary sprigs, to garnish

double cream, to garnish

white soda bread (see page 228), to serve

SERVES 4

Roasted Red Pepper & Sun-dried Tomato Soup

Follow this recipe for a spicy twist on the simple traditional tomato soup.

METHOD

Preheat the oven to 200°C/400°F/Gas Mark 6. Place the peppers onion halves (cut side down) and garlic cloves on a baking tray and drizzle with the oil. Bake in the preheated oven for 30 minutes or until the vegetables are tender.

Meanwhile, put the butter into a large saucepan over a medium heat and heat until melted. Add the celery and sauté for 4–5 minutes. Add the stock, tomato purée and chilli flakes and mix well to combine. Remove from the heat.

Peel the onion and the garlic cloves, then chop them and add to the pan with the canned tomatoes. Heat over a low–medium heat until just simmering, then blend until smooth. Season to taste with salt and pepper.

Divide the soup among four warmed bowls, garnish with a swi of cream and some fresh rosemary and serve immediately with white soda bread.

INGREDIENTS

25 g/1 oz butter
1 onion, finely chopped
1 potato, diced
1 litre/1¾ pints ham stock
500 g/1 lb 2 oz frozen peas
300 g/10½ oz lean cooked ham, coarsely shredded

Pea & Ham Soup

Ham always works well with peas and it makes this soup a meal in itself, especially if eaten with fresh bread and washed down with a pint of Guinness.

METHOD

Put the butter into a large saucepan and heat over a medium heat until foaming. Add the onions and cook for 5–6 minutes until softened. Add the potato and stir to coat in the butter.

Add the stock and simmer, uncovered, until the potato is soft. Add the peas and bring to the boil. Cook for 1–2 minutes, then transfer the soup to a food processor and process until smooth. Stir in the ham.

Divide the soup among four warmed bowls and serve immediately.

SERVES 4

INGREDIENTS

2 tbsp olive oil
2 garlic cloves, finely chopped
2 tbsp finely chopped fresh basil
1 kg/2 lb 4 oz courgettes, cut into 1-cm/½-inch slices
750 ml/1¼ pints vegetable stock
100 ml/3½ fl oz milk
55 g/2 oz grated Parmesan cheese, plus extra to serve
salt and freshly ground black pepper
double cream, to garnish

Creamy Courgette Soup

An unusual soup that the makes good use of a summer glut of courgettes.

METHOD

Heat the oil in a large saucepan over a medium heat. Add the garlic, basil and courgettes, season to taste with salt and cook for 10 minutes, until the courgettes are soft. Reserve some of the courgette pieces to garnish.

Add the stock and simmer for 5 minutes, uncovered, then add the milk and bring just to a simmer. Season with pepper.

Transfer the soup to a food processor and process until smooth then return to the pan and stir in the cheese.

Divide the soup among four warmed bowls, garnish with the reserved courgette pieces and a swirl of cream. Serve immediately.

SERVES 4

INGREDIENTS

1 blade of mace
1 bouquet garni
2 tbsp bacon fat or butter
1 large potato, peeled and chopped
1 onion, chopped
4 carrots, chopped
3 celery sticks, chopped
1.7 litres/3 pints vegetable stock
55 g/2 oz brown lentils
30 g/1 oz ground rice
125 ml/4 fl oz milk
125 ml/4 fl oz cream
salt and freshly ground black pepper
fresh parsley sprigs, to garnish

Potato & Vegetable Soup

The mace in this recipe helps to bring out the earthy flavours of the root vegetables, lifting this otherwise very simple soup out of the ordinary.

METHOD

Add the mace to the bouquet garni. Melt the fat in a saucepan, add the vegetables, and toss. Cook gently until they have absorbed the fat but are not browned.

Add the stock and the lentils, bring to the boil and simmer for 45 minutes. Remove the bouquet garni and liquidise.

Return to the saucepan and thicken with the ground rice. Season with salt and pepper, then add the milk and cream and bring back to the boil. Serve in warmed bowls, garnished with parsley sprigs.

SERVES 6

The Galway Oyster Festival

The oyster, that succulent bivalve mollusc that is so abundant on the Irish coastline, has been a popular food for centuries, particularly when it was cheap to buy or even free to gather for those lucky enough to live by the sea. Nowadays, it is no longer part of the daily diet and has attained mythical status as an aphrodisiac. It is celebrated in Ireland in several festivals that are dedicated to it, none more famous, or older, than the Galway International Oyster and Seafood Festival.

The three-day festival is held every year over the last weekend of September – September traditionally being the first month of the oyster season, obeying the proscription on eating oysters (and all shellfish) in any month without an 'r' in its name. The season ends in April.

The festival was founded in 1954, and it attracted 300 people in its first year. It is now a popular event in the county's calendar, bringing up to 25,000 people from far and wide to sample the briny oysters (and to wash them down with their perfect taste

complement, Guinness) and to enjoy all the craic that Galway has to offer.

The opening ceremony is the presentation of the first oyster of the season to the Mayor of Galway by the newly crowned festival queen, the Oyster Pearl. While this is a festival of food and drink, with all the local bars and restaurants rising to the occasion with delicious seafood-centred menus, the main event is the World Oyster Opening Championship. This is sponsored by Guinness and is an oyster-shucking time trial – the skilled shucker who opens 30 oysters in the shortest time is declared the winner.

With live music, international food offerings, a gala mardi gras and a best-dressed lady competition, there's something for everyone – or you can just enjoy a few oysters.

INGREDIENTS

600 ml/1 pint water
1 bay leaf
juice of 1 lemon
550 g/1 lb 4 oz
smoked haddock, cut
into large chunks
2 tbsp butter
1 small onion, finely
chopped
225 g/8 oz button
mushrooms, sliced
1 tbsp plain flour
425 ml/15 fl oz hot
milk
freshly ground black
pepper
chopped fresh
parsley, to garnish

Smoked Haddock & Mushroom Chowder

This hearty soup is best enjoyed with fresh bread and Irish butter.

METHOD

Bring the water to the boil in a large saucepan, then add the bay leaf, lemon juice and fish, season to taste with pepper and poach for 5 minutes.

Transfer the fish to a plate and set aside, reserving the poaching liquid.

Melt the butter in a separate large saucepan, add the onion and mushrooms and sauté until softened. Add the flour and mix well.

Gradually add the milk and the reserved poaching liquid, stirring constantly, until the desired consistency is achieved.

Return the fish to the pan and reheat over a low heat.

Serve the chowder in warmed bowl, garnished with parsley.

SERVES 6

INGREDIENTS

225 ml/8 fl oz fresh fish stock

1 small white onion, diced

1 celery stick, diced

125 ml/4 fl oz Irish stout

450 g/1 lb potatoes, peeled and diced

1 tsp fresh thyme

24 fresh oysters, carefully removed from their shells

125 ml/4 fl oz milk

freshly ground black pepper

chopped fresh watercress or parsley, to garnish

Galway Oyster Bisque

A rich and luxurious soup for a special occasion, traditionally served in pubs at the Galway Oyster Festival every September.

METHOD

Heat 2 tablespoons of the stock in a large saucepan. Add the onion and celery and cook over a medium heat until translucent. Add the stout, the remaining stock, the potatoes and thyme, bring to the boil and cook until the potatoes are softened.

Transfer to a blender, add the oysters and the milk, then add pepper to taste and blend until smooth.

Return to the pan and bring to the boil.

Serve in warmed bowls, garnished with some watercress or parsley.

SERVES 4

INGREDIENTS

1 kg/2 lb 4 oz
Dublin Bay prawns,
shell on

2 onions, thinly
sliced

300 ml/10 fl oz
olive oil

1 tbsp brandy

1 chicken stock cube

200 ml/7 fl oz water

1 tsp sugar

2 tbsp finely
chopped fresh
parsley

salt and freshly
ground black pepper

Dublin Bay Prawns

Otherwise known as langoustines, these delicious crustaceans are best cooked and served shell on.

METHOD

Remove the legs and whiskers from the prawns and wash the shellfish under cold running water.

Put the onions into a colander and pour over a little boiling water.

Heat the oil in a large saucepan, add the onions and sauté until translucent. Add the prawns and sauté, then add the brandy.

Crumble in the stock cube, then add the water, sugar and parsley and season with salt and pepper. Bring to the boil, then simmer for 2–3 minutes.

Serve immediately in warmed bowls.

SERVES 4

INGREDIENTS

250 g/9 oz smoked
mackerel, skinned

125 g/4½ oz cream
cheese

1 tbsp chopped fresh
dill or basil

oatcakes (see page
230) or brown soda
bread (see page
224) and butter, to
serve

Smoked Mackerel Pâté

This simple starter is delicious spread on
oatcakes or brown soda bread and butter.

METHOD

Put the mackerel and cream cheese into a food processor and
process until smooth. Stir in some fresh dill or basil. Pack the
mixture into four ramekins and chill for at least 2–3 hours.

Stir in the dill or basil and serve in the ramekins with oatcakes

SERVES 4

INGREDIENTS

36 large cooked,
peeled prawns
mixed salad leaves
lemon wedges, to
serve

Marie Rose sauce
2 tbsp double cream
2 tbsp mayonnaise
2 tbsp tomato
ketchup
1 tsp lemon juice
1 tsp sweet sherry
dash of
Worcestershire sauce
salt and freshly
ground black pepper

Prawn Cocktail

This starter was popular in the 1970s and has come right back into fashion.

METHOD

To make the sauce, whip the cream until soft peaks form, then beat in the remaining ingredients. Chill for 1 hour.

Arrange the salad leaves in the base of six glasses. Add six prawns to each glass and drizzle over the sauce, leaving a prawn or two to decorate the top.

Serve immediately with lemon wedges.

SERVES 6

INGREDIENTS

55 g/2 oz butter

55 g/2 oz plain flour

150 ml/5 fl oz milk

225 g/8 oz smoked haddock, cooked and flaked

225 g/8 oz mashed potatoes

1 tbsp chopped fresh dill

1 egg, beaten

6 tbsp dried golden breadcrumbs

vegetable oil, for frying

salt and freshly ground black pepper

tartare sauce and lemon wedges, to serve

Smoked Haddock Fishcakes

Serve these delicious fishcakes as a substantial starter or a light lunch dish.

METHOD

Melt the butter in a saucepan over a medium heat, then stir in the flour and cook for 1 minute. Gradually add the milk and cook, stirring constantly, until thickened.

Remove from the heat and leave to cool, then add the fish and potatoes with salt and pepper to taste and mix with the dill to combine. Shape the mixture into eight cakes.

Beat the egg with a fork in a wide shallow dish. Put the breadcrumbs on a plate. Dip the cakes in the beaten egg and then in the breadcrumbs, turning to coat.

Heat some oil in frying pan, then add the cakes and fry for 5 minutes on each side until golden brown.

Drain on kitchen paper and serve immediately with tartare sauce and lemon wedges.

SERVES 4

INGREDIENTS

6 streaky bacon
rashers

12 scallops, corals
removed

3 tbsp fresh lemon
juice

lemon wedges, to
serve

Scallops Wrapped in Bacon

A classic *amuse bouche* that couldn't be
easier to prepare. Use Parma ham for a
luxury version.

METHOD

Preheat the oven to 180°C/350°F/Gas Mark 4.

Cut the bacon slices in half and wrap each piece around a
scallop, securing with cocktail sticks.

Drizzle the lemon juice over the scallops, then place on a
baking tray and bake in the preheated oven for 15–20 minutes
until the bacon is crisp and sizzling. Serve warm, with lemon
wedges for squeezing over.

MAKES 12

INGREDIENTS

24 fresh oysters
ice, lemon wedges
and brown soda
bread (see page
224), to serve

Festival Oysters

These can quickly become addictive,
especially when washed down with a pint
of the black stuff.

METHOD

Wash the oysters, discarding any that are slightly open. Open
the oysters using an oyster knife, reserving any shell juices.

Arrange the ice on chilled plates and place the oysters on top,
in their shells. Drizzle over the reserved juices.

Serve immediately with lemon wedges and brown soda bread.

SERVES 4

INGREDIENTS

20 raw Dublin Bay prawns, peeled and deveined

30 g/1 oz plain flour

pinch of cayenne pepper

85 g/3 oz fresh white breadcrumbs

1 large egg, beaten

vegetable oil, for frying

salt and freshly ground black pepper

lemon wedges and tartare sauce, to serve

Golden Scampi

This favourite pub offering is a delicious showcase for the world-renowned Dublin Bay prawns.

METHOD

Rinse the prawns and pat dry with kitchen paper. Line a plate with baking paper.

Put the flour into a bowl, add the cayenne pepper and season taste with salt and pepper. Spread the breadcrumbs on a wide plate. Beat the egg with a fork in a wide shallow dish.

Roll each prawn in the flour mixture, then dip in the beaten e and roll in the breadcrumbs to coat. Transfer to the prepared plate.

Heat the oil in a large, high-sided frying pan to 180°C/350°F, or until a cube of bread dropped into the oil turns golden and crisp in 30 seconds.

Add the scampi to the oil in batches and cook for 3 minutes. Remove with a slotted spoon and drain on kitchen paper.

Serve immediately with lemon wedges and tartare sauce. You could also serve the scampi with peas and chips for a more substantial meal.

SERVES 4

INGREDIENTS

48 large mussels

300 ml/10 fl oz Irish stout

225 g/8 oz butter, at room temperature

10 garlic cloves, crushed

100 g/3½ oz fresh white breadcrumbs

2 tbsp chopped fresh parsley

lemon wedges and crusty bread, to serve

Stuffed Mussels

This is an Irish variation on mussels steamed in wine – stout is the perfect partner for shellfish.

METHOD

Clean the mussels under cold running water and pull off the beards, discarding any mussels that are open or that refuse to close when tapped.

Put the mussels into a large saucepan with the stout and a little water and heat until the mussels have opened. Drain the mussels and discard any that remain closed. Remove the top shell of each mussel.

Meanwhile, mix the butter and garlic together, then add the breadcrumbs and parsley and mix to combine. Preheat the grill to high.

Place some of the mixture on each mussel and cook under the hot grill for 5–10 minutes until sizzling.

Serve immediately with lemon wedges and crusty bread.

SERVES 4-6

INGREDIENTS

1 cooked lobster, meat
removed and cut into
bite-sized pieces

1 cooked crab, meat
removed and cut into
bite-sized pieces

1 kg/2 lb 4 oz
cooked tiger prawns,
unpeeled

24 oysters

Sweet chilli dip

2 green chillies,
roughly chopped

2 garlic cloves,
roughly chopped

2 tbsp Thai fish sauce

2 tbsp palm sugar

large handful fresh
coriander leaves

4 tbsp fresh lime juice

Mayonnaise dip

150 ml/5 fl oz
mayonnaise

1 tbsp finely chopped
fresh dill

finely grated rind and
juice of 1 lime

SERVES 8

Seafood Platter

This is a great sharing platter – for
maximum impact, arrange the lobster and
crabmeat in their shells.

METHOD

To make the sweet chilli dip, put all the ingredients into a
food processor and process until almost smooth. Transfer to a
serving bowl.

To make the mayonnaise dip, put all the ingredients in a serving
bowl and stir to combine.

Cover a large serving platter with crushed ice. Arrange the
lobster, crab, prawns and oysters on the ice. Serve with the
dipping sauces.

INGREDIENTS

500 g/1 lb 2 oz hot-smoked salmon

500 g/1 lb 2 oz smoked trout

500 g/1 lb 2 oz smoked mackerel

24 smoked mussels, on the shell

24 smoked oysters, on the shell

24 lemon wedges, to garnish

To serve

brown soda bread (see page 224) and butter

cooked beetroot

gherkins

aïoli (see page 58)

Smoked Fish Platter

Smoked fish is available all year round from excellent Irish producers. Use wild fish, wherever possible.

METHOD

Arrange all the ingredients on a large platter and scatter over the lemon wedges.

Serve immediately with bread and butter and dishes of beetroot, gherkins and aïoli.

SERVES 12

INGREDIENTS

1 head iceberg lettuce

125 ml/4 fl oz bottled Italian salad dressing

250 g/9 oz Parma ham, thinly sliced

450 g/1 lb Taleggio cheese, sliced

225 g/8 oz salami, sliced

100 g/3½ oz cooked ham, sliced

175 g/6 oz bottled artichoke hearts

300 g/10½ oz roasted red peppers in olive oil, drained

200 g/7 oz green olives

200 g/7 oz black olives

300 g/10½ oz mozzarella cheese, sliced

chopped fresh parsley and basil, to garnish

fresh ciabatta, to serve

SERVES 10

Italian Antipasti Platter

A delicious collection of Italian antipasti ingredients. You'll probably have most of them to hand, so this is a great last-minute dish when friends arrive unexpectedly.

METHOD

Tear the lettuce leaves and arrange them on the base of a large serving platter. Drizzle with the dressing, then arrange the remaining ingredients attractively on top, finishing with a garnish of chopped parsley and basil.

Serve immediately with sliced ciabatta.

INGREDIENTS

400 g/14 oz mature Irish red Cheddar cheese

400 g/14 oz Gubbeen cheese or a cheese such as Ruby Irish ale cheese from Cooleeney Farm

400 g/14 oz vintage Irish Cheddar

400 g/14 oz Cashel Blue cheese

400 g/14 oz Carrigbyrne or an Irish soft cheese such as the Little Milk Company's organic Irish Brie

To serve

fig chutney

quince jelly

grapes

crunchy savoury oatcakes (see page 230)

cheese & herb crackers (see page 232)

SERVES 12

Irish Cheese Platter

Delicious Irish cheeses are justifiably famous. There are many artisan cheeses made in Ireland, such as Gubbeen, Milleens, Durrus, Carrigbyrne and Cooleeney. A combination of hard, soft, mild and strong is sure to be a crowd-pleaser, but you can use any cheese you like. Always serve cheese at room temperature.

METHOD

Arrange all the cheeses on a marble or slate platter or a large board and serve with accompaniments of your choice.

INGREDIENTS

250 g/9 oz French beans, trimmed

250 g/9 oz asparagus

250 g/9 oz cauliflower florets

250 g/9 oz mange tout

1 red and 1 yellow pepper, cut into strips

12 radishes

12 spring onions

150 g/5½ oz cherry tomatoes

6 carrots, cut into sticks

2 small courgettes, cut into sticks

1 cucumber, cut into sticks

Aïoli

6 garlic cloves, crushed

4 egg yolks

2 tbsp Dijon mustard

600 ml/1 pint extra virgin olive oil

4 tsp lemon juice

salt and freshly ground black pepper

SERVES 10-12

Vegetable Platter with Aïoli

A colourful platter of crunchy vegetables – delicious when dipped in smooth, garlick aïoli. This is the perfect summer snack for a small gathering.

METHOD

To make the aïoli, put the garlic, egg yolks and mustard into a food processor and blitz until smooth and combined. Very slowly add the oil, pulsing after each addition, until a thick mayonnaise-style sauce forms. Add the lemon juice, then seaso to taste with salt and pepper. Cover and chill for up to 2 days.

Bring a large saucepan of salted water to the boil and fill a larg bowl with iced water. Drop the beans into the boiling water and cook for 2 minutes, then scoop them out of the water and immediately plunge them into the iced water. Remove them from the water and pat dry. Repeat with the asparagus and cauliflower.

Arrange all the vegetables on a large serving platter and serve with the aïoli.

INGREDIENTS

8 smoked streaky bacon rashers, chopped

500 g/1 lb 2 oz mashed potatoes

1 tbsp snipped fresh chives

100 g/3½ oz blue cheese

2 tbsp thick natural yogurt

30 g/1 oz plain flour, for dusting

1½ tbsp vegetable oil

freshly ground black pepper

Smoked Bacon & Potato Cakes

These potato cakes are a delicious way of using up yesterday's mashed potato.

METHOD

Place the bacon in a dry frying pan and fry over a high heat un crisp. Set aside.

Put the potatoes, chives, cheese, yogurt and pepper to taste in a bowl and mix well to combine. Add the bacon and mix. Divi the mixture into four equal portions and shape each portion into a small cake. Chill for 30 minutes.

Spread the flour on a plate and turn the cakes in it to coat.

Heat the oil in a large frying pan, add the potato cakes and fry for 5 minutes on each side until golden and cooked through. Serve hot.

SERVES 4

INGREDIENTS

675 g/1 lb 8 oz
chicken livers
125 ml/4 fl oz
brandy
125 ml/4 fl oz
sweet sherry
250 g/9 oz butter,
plus extra for
greasing
1 shallot, finely
chopped
4 garlic cloves, very
finely chopped
3 fresh thyme sprigs
125 ml/4 fl oz
double cream
2 large eggs
salt and freshly
ground black pepper
chopped fresh
parsley, to garnish

Chicken Liver Pâté

This rich, creamy pâté is delicious served
with toast or brown soda bread, with a
little fig chutney on the side.

METHOD

Put the chicken livers in a bowl with the brandy, sherry and salt
and pepper to taste. Cover and chill for 12 hours.

The next day, preheat the oven to 180°C/325°F/Gas Mark 4.
Grease a 900-g/2-lb loaf tin and line with baking paper, leaving a
generous overhang to fold over the pâté.

Put 2 tablespoons of the butter into a small frying pan and heat
until melted. Add the shallot, garlic and thyme and cook for 3–4
minutes until softened but not browned. Remove from the heat
discard the thyme and leave to cool. Melt the remaining butter i
a saucepan, then remove from the heat and leave to cool.

Put the chicken liver mixture into a food processor with the oni
mixture, the cooled butter, cream and eggs. Process for 15–20
seconds, or until smooth. Carefully spoon into the prepared tin
then cover with the baking paper and place in a deep roasting t
Add hot water to halfway up the side of the loaf tin.

Bake in the preheated oven for 1 hour–1 hour 15 minutes, or
until the top is slightly firm. Remove from the oven, transfer to
a wire rack and leave to cool completely before serving with a
garnish of chopped parsley.

SERVES 4

INGREDIENTS

vegetable oil, for frying

4 large rounds black pudding

2 tbsp butter

1 tsp caster sugar

1 Bramley apple, cored and cut into rings

Black Pudding with Fried Apple Rings

This is a filling starter – if you double the quantities it would make a good main course, served with red cabbage.

METHOD

Heat some oil in a frying pan, add the black pudding and fry for 4–5 minutes on each side until cooked through.

Meanwhile, melt the butter in a separate frying pan over a high heat, add the sugar and the apple rings and fry for 4–5 minutes until golden brown and slightly caramelised.

Arrange the black pudding on warmed plates with the apple rings. Drizzle over any caramelised pan juices and serve immediately.

SERVES 2

INGREDIENTS

150 g/5½ oz seasoned plain flour

4 eggs, lightly beaten

300 g/10½ oz fresh white breadcrumbs

400 g/14 oz Irish Camembert-style cheese (1 round)

vegetable oil, for deep-frying

Redcurrant sauce

300 g/10½ oz redcurrants, stalks removed

150 g/5½ oz soft light brown sugar

3 tbsp red wine vinegar

Deep-fried Irish Camembert with Redcurrant Sauce

This is a delicious starter or canapé, perfectly complemented by the zingy redcurrant sauce.

METHOD

To make the sauce, put all the ingredients into a saucepan over a medium heat and bring to the boil. Reduce the heat and simmer for about 20 minutes until the redcurrants are soft and giving off their juices. Remove from the heat and set aside.

Put the flour, eggs and breadcrumbs into three separate bowls.

Cut the cheese into nine pieces. Dip into the flour to coat, then into the beaten egg. Roll in the breadcrumbs to coat completely. Dip again into the egg and breadcrumbs.

Meanwhile, heat enough oil for deep-frying in a large saucepan until a cube of bread dropped into it browns in 30 seconds. Add the cheese to the pan and deep-fry, turning occasionally, until crisp and golden.

Remove from the pan with a slotted spoon and transfer to kitchen paper to drain.

Serve hot with the redcurrant sauce.

SERVES 6

INGREDIENTS

2 slices brown bread

25 g/1 oz butter, softened

2 thick slices cold roast pork, trimmed of fat

100 g/3½ oz chutney

55 g/2 oz pickled onions

Roast Pork, Chutney & Pickled Onion Open Sandwich

This is a delicious way of using up the Sunday roast – it needs a really good brown bread.

METHOD

Spread the butter on the bread slices and place a slice of pork on each. Top with the chutney, scatter over a few pickled onio and serve.

SERVES 1

INGREDIENTS

4 tbsp aïoli (see page 58)

4 slices sourdough bread, toasted

2 avocados, stoned and thickly sliced

8 large cooked peeled prawns, halved

mild paprika, to garnish

Prawn & Avocado Open Sandwich

A delicious combination of smooth avocado and firm cooked prawns on substantial sourdough toast.

METHOD

Spread the aïoli on the toast and arrange the avocado slices on top. Divide the prawns among the sandwiches and garnish with a little paprika. Serve immediately.

SERVES 2–4

INGREDIENTS

200 g/7 oz cream cheese

4 slices brown soda bread (see page 224)

150 g/5½ oz smoked salmon slices

½ cucumber, very finely sliced

freshly ground black pepper

chopped fresh parsley, to garnish

Smoked Salmon, Cream Cheese & Cucumber Open Sandwich

The classic combination of cucumber, cream cheese and smoked salmon on brown soda bread makes a delicious and very satisfying sandwich.

METHOD

Spread the cream cheese on the bread and arrange the smoke salmon slices on top. Cover with the cucumber slices and season to taste with pepper. Garnish with parsley and serve immediately.

SERVES 2–4

INGREDIENTS

125 g/4½ oz soft goat's cheese

100 g/3½ oz crème fraîche

2 garlic cloves, very finely chopped

1 tbsp chopped fresh tarragon, plus extra to garnish

1 small ciabatta loaf, halved lengthways

4 cooked beetroot, sliced

125 g/4½ oz baby spinach leaves

salt and freshly ground black pepper

Beetroot, Goat's Cheese & Baby Spinach Open Sandwich

The earthy flavour of the beetroot is complemented by the creamy cheese base. You could use rocket instead of baby beetroot for a peppery touch.

METHOD

Put the cheese, crème fraîche, garlic and tarragon into a bowl and mix with a fork until combined.

Spread the cheese mixture on the cut surfaces of the bread and arrange the beetroot slices on top.

Put the spinach into a sieve and pour over some boiling water to wilt. Pat dry with kitchen paper, then divide between the sandwiches. Season to taste with salt and pepper, garnish with tarragon and serve.

SERVES 2

MAIN DISHES

INGREDIENTS

4 large potatoes, peeled and thickly sliced

450 g/1 lb sausages, each sliced into 4 or 5 pieces

450 g/1 lb streaky bacon, cut into small pieces

2 onions, roughly chopped

1 tbsp chopped fresh parsley

300 ml/10 fl oz water

salt and freshly ground black pepper

Dublin Coddle

A hearty and economical winter stew, full of warming flavour, made with sausages and streaky bacon.

METHOD

Layer the potatoes, sausages, bacon and onions in a large saucepan, adding salt and pepper to each layer and finishing with a potato layer and a little parsley.

Add the water, then bring to the boil over a medium heat. Reduce the heat and simmer for at least 1 hour.

Stir in the parsley and serve in warmed bowls.

SERVES 4

INGREDIENTS

1 kg/2 lb 4 oz
middle neck of lamb,
trimmed and cut into
chunks

4 large potatoes,
peeled and sliced

2 carrots, sliced

2 onions, sliced

500 ml/18 fl oz
water

salt and freshly
ground black pepper

chopped fresh
parsley, to garnish

Irish Stew

This very simple dish was originally a
white stew made with an economical
mutton cut. Nowadays, carrots are often
added for colour and flavour and lamb ha
replaced the mutton.

METHOD

Preheat the oven to 160°C/325°F/Gas Mark 3.

Layer the meat, potatoes, carrots and onions in a casserole dish
adding salt and pepper to each layer and finishing with a layer
of potatoes.

Add the water, cover with a tight-fitting lid and cook in the
preheated oven for at least 2 hours.

Serve in warmed bowls, garnished with parsley.

SERVES 4

INGREDIENTS

1 tbsp vegetable oil

450 g/1 lb stewing beef, trimmed and cut into chunks

plain flour seasoned with salt, freshly ground black pepper and ground ginger, for dusting

400 g/14 oz canned chopped tomatoes

1 tbsp red wine vinegar

3 tbsp sweet chilli sauce

1 tbsp soft light brown sugar

1 tbsp Worcestershire sauce

1 garlic clove, finely chopped

1 bay leaf

1 red and 1 yellow pepper, deseeded and cut into chunks

fresh parsley sprigs, to garnish

SERVES 4

Sweet & Spicy Beef

The subtle balance of spicy and sweet flavours makes this a hearty and warming dish. Serve with rice or mashed potato.

METHOD

Preheat the oven to 180°C/350°F/Gas Mark 4.

Heat the oil in a large frying pan. Toss the beef in the seasoned flour, add to the pan and cook until browned all over. Remove from the pan and place in the base of an ovenproof dish.

Whizz the tomatoes, vinegar, chilli sauce, sugar, Worcestershire sauce and garlic in a blender or food processor. Pour over the meat, add the bay leaf and bake in the preheated oven for at least 1 hour.

Add the red and yellow peppers and return to the oven for a further 30 minutes, until the meat and peppers are tender.

Remove the bay leaf and discard. Serve in warmed bowls, garnished with parsley.

The Guinness Harp

'Queen of Musick you may call me', reads the inscription on the 1702 Downhill Harp, displayed in the Guinness Storehouse in Dublin.

Think of a drink in connection with Dublin's fair city and you'll almost inevitably come up with Guinness, the famous black stout first brewed by Arthur Guinness from barley, hops, yeast and water back in 1759. If you ask anyone what the Guinness label looks like, they'll tell you that it has a harp. The oval beige label, featuring a harp and Arthur Guinness's signature, is probably one of the most enduring and recognisable trademarks in the world.

Guinness first used the emblem of the Irish harp on its labelling in 1862. Prior to that, the stout was sold in barrels and bottled by the public houses where it was sold. However, because a practice of mixing beers developed, Guinness decided that the bottles containing its stout should be clearly labelled, and publicans undertook not to mix it with any other product. The harp was registered in London as the brewery's trademark in 1876, one of the first marks to be registered to a brewery.

The harp on the Guinness label is based on the famous Trinty College harp, the Brian Boru harp. The first labels had 'trademark' printed on the soundboard of the harp, but subsequent modifications – there have been many – omitted this and the current Guinness harp is much simpler than the original highly decorated version.

The Irish harp is also the emblem of Ireland – it appears on all government documents, including passports. In 1922, because of the Guinness trademark, the Irish Free State government decided to face the official Irish harp in the opposite direction, so the Guinness harp has the soundboard on the left, while the harp in the government emblem shows it on the right.

And the story of the Guinness harp doesn't end there – in 1960 the brewery decided to launch its first lager beer called, simply, Harp.

INGREDIENTS

85 g/3 oz butter

1 onion, finely chopped

2 garlic cloves, finely chopped

900 g/2 lb stewing beef, trimmed and cut into chunks

2 tbsp seasoned flour

115 g/4 oz carrots, thickly sliced

55 g/2 oz celery, thickly sliced

¼ tsp grated nutmeg

¼ tsp mixed spice

600 ml/1 pint Guinness

grated zest and juice of 2 oranges

salt and freshly ground black pepper

chopped fresh parsley, to garnish

SERVES 4-6

Zesty Beef & Guinness Casserole

This recipe tastes better if made the day before eating, so it's perfect for entertaining. Serve with lots of creamy mashed potato.

METHOD

Preheat the oven to 120°C/250°F/Gas Mark ½.

Melt half the butter in a casserole dish, add the onion and garlic and sweat over a low heat for 10 minutes, or until softened.

Meanwhile toss the meat in the seasoned flour. Melt the remaining butter in a large frying pan, add the meat and cook, tossing occasionally, until browned all over. Transfer to the casserole dish.

Add the carrots, celery, nutmeg and mixed spice to the casserole dish, season to taste with salt and pepper and pour in the Guinness. Bring to a simmer, then cover with a tight-fitting lid and cook in the preheated oven for about 6 hours, until the meat is meltingly tender. Stir in the orange zest and juice and leave to cool overnight.

Reheat in an oven preheated to 150°C/300°F/Gas Mark 2 for 45 minutes. Serve in warmed bowls, garnished with parsley.

INGREDIENTS

1 tbsp seasoned flour

900 g/2 lb best quality beef steak, cut into small pieces

85 g/3 oz butter

8 streaky bacon rashers, chopped

5 onions, chopped

1 tbsp raisins

1 tsp soft light brown sugar

300 ml/10 fl oz Irish stout

450 g/1 lb ready-rolled shortcrust pastry

beaten egg, for glazing

Steak & Stout Pie

Beef and stout blend perfectly in this delicious pie. The crust is broken open to reveal a rich, dark interior.

METHOD

Put the seasoned flour in a large bowl, add the beef and toss to coat. Melt the butter in a frying pan, then add the beef and the bacon and cook, stirring occasionally, until browned.

Transfer the meat to a casserole dish. Add the onions to the pan and fry until golden. Add to the casserole with the raisins, sugar and stout.

Cover tightly, bring to the boil over a medium heat, then reduce the heat and simmer for about 2 hours until the meat is tender, adding more liquid if needed.

Meanwhile, preheat the oven to 200°C/400°F/Gas Mark 6. Transfer the contents of the casserole dish to a deep pie dish and cover with the pastry, trimming and sealing the edges. Brush with the beaten egg and cook in the preheated oven for 30–35 minutes, until golden brown.

Serve hot.

SERVES 4

INGREDIENTS

2 kg/4 lb 8 oz
Limerick ham joint

200 g/7 oz Dijon
mustard

25 cloves

300 g/10½ oz
molasses sugar or
soft dark brown
sugar

200 ml/7 fl oz clear
honey

Parsley sauce

4 tbsp butter

3 tbsp plain flour

300 ml/10 fl oz hot
milk

30 g/1 oz chopped
fresh parsley, or to
taste

salt and freshly
ground black pepper

SERVES 6-8

Baked Limerick Ham with Parsley Sauce

Limerick ham is the king of Irish ham. The parsley sauce is the perfect accompaniment.

METHOD

Put the ham into a large saucepan and cover with cold water. Bring to the boil over a medium heat, then reduce the heat and simmer for 1–1½ hours, skimming off any foam, until the meat is tender. Remove from the heat and leave to stand for 30 minutes.

Meanwhile, preheat the oven to 160°C/325°F/Gas Mark 3. Remove the ham from the cooking liquid and transfer to a large roasting tin. Use a sharp knife to score the fat in a diamond pattern, then coat with the mustard and stick a clove in each diamond. Sprinkle with the sugar and drizzle over the honey.

Bake in the preheated oven for 30–35 minutes, or until the crust is golden. Remove from the oven and leave to stand for 2 minutes.

Meanwhile, to make the sauce, melt the butter in a small saucepan over a medium heat. Gradually stir in the flour and cook for 10 minutes until a paste forms. Slowly add the milk, whisking constantly, until thickened and smooth. Season to taste with salt and pepper and stir in the parsley.

INGREDIENTS

1 half leg of Wicklow
lamb, fillet end,
about 2 kg/4 lb 8 oz
2 garlic cloves,
peeled and sliced
leaves of 1 large
fresh rosemary sprig
salt and freshly
ground black pepper
roast potatoes (see
page 156) and
minted peas (see
page 162), to serve

Gravy
2 tbsp plain flour
125 ml/4 fl oz lamb
or beef stock
125 ml/4 fl oz red
wine

Roast Wicklow Lamb

Wicklow lamb is Ireland's pride. Delicately
flavoured with rosemary and garlic, this is
the traditional Easter Sunday lunch joint.

METHOD

Preheat the oven to 230°C/450°F/Gas Mark 8. Put the lamb on a
rack in a deep roasting tin. Using a sharp knife, make 1-cm/½-
inch deep slits in the skin of the joint.

Rub salt and pepper all over the skin, then insert the garlic
slices and rosemary into the slits.

Roast in the preheated oven for 30 minutes, then reduce the
heat to 180°C/350°F/Gas Mark 4 and roast for a further 30
minutes per 450 g/1 lb. Remove from the oven and leave to rest.

To make the gravy, pour off most of the fat from the tin, then
sprinkle the flour over the remaining sediment. Whisk over a
medium heat until smooth, then gradually whisk in the stock
and wine. Bring to the boil and bubble until reduced and
thickened.

Carve the lamb into slices and serve on warmed plates with the
gravy, roast potatoes and peas.

SERVES 4

INGREDIENTS

butter, for greasing

plain flour, for dusting

250 g/9 oz ready-made shortcrust pastry

6 streaky bacon rashers, chopped

4 large eggs

½ tsp salt

¼ tsp freshly ground black pepper

100 g/3½ oz mature Cheddar cheese, coarsely grated

1 red onion, roughly chopped

1 large tomato, thinly sliced

fresh thyme sprig, to garnish

SERVES 4-6

Quiche Lorraine

Introduced here in the 1960s, this was the first quiche to achieve popularity in Ireland. It makes a delicious lunch dish.

METHOD

Preheat the oven to 220°C/425°F/Gas Mark 7. Grease a 23-cm/9 inch round flan tin.

Roll out the pastry on a work surface lightly dusted with flour t a round 5 cm/2 inches larger than the diameter of the tin. Use the pastry to line the tin, then trim so that it is 2.5 cm/1 inch higher than the top of the tin. Line with baking paper, fill with baking beans and bake in the preheated oven for 10 minutes. Remove the paper and beans and bake for a further 2 minutes.

Meanwhile, add the bacon to a hot frying pan and fry until cooked to your liking, then cut into small pieces. Beat the eggs with the salt and pepper.

Remove the pastry case from the oven and reduce the oven temperature to 160°C/325°F/Gas Mark 3. Sprinkle the bacon, most of the cheese and the onion into the pastry case. Pour in the egg mixture and sprinkle with the remaining cheese.

Arrange the tomato slices on top, return to the oven and bake for a further 45–50 minutes, or until a skewer inserted into th centre comes out clean. Garnish with thyme and serve warm o cold.

INGREDIENTS

butter, for greasing
flour, for dusting
250 g/9 oz ready-made shortcrust pastry
1 tbsp olive oil
1 onion, roughly chopped
200 g/7 oz cherry tomatoes
1 tsp sugar
5 large eggs
1 tsp chopped fresh sage
200 g/7 oz soft goat's cheese, chopped fresh
chopped fresh parsley
salt and freshly ground black pepper

SERVES 4

Caramelised Cherry Tomato & Goat's Cheese Tart

This is a good option for lunch, and is delicious served either warm or cold.

METHOD

Preheat the oven to 220°C/425°F/Gas Mark 7. Grease a 23-cm/9-inch round flan tin.

Roll out the pastry on a work surface lightly dusted with flour to a round 5 cm/2 inches larger than the diameter of the tin. Use to line the tin, prick with a fork, then line with baking paper and baking beans and bake in the preheated oven for 10 minutes. Remove the paper and beans and bake for a further 2 minutes.

Meanwhile, heat the oil in a frying pan over a medium heat, then add the onion and cook until softened. Add the tomatoes and cook until soft and beginning to burst, then stir in the sugar and cook for a further 5 minutes, until the tomatoes are lightly caramelised.

Meanwhile, beat the eggs with the sage and some salt and pepper.

Remove the pastry case from the oven and reduce the oven temperature to 160°C/325°F/Gas Mark 3. Carefully pour the tomato mixture over the base of the pastry case and scatter over the cheese, making sure that the cheese and tomatoes are evenly distributed. Pour in the egg mixture and scatter the parsley on top.

Return to the oven and bake for 30–35 minutes until the egg is set.

Leave to cool for 5 minutes. Serve warm or cold.

INGREDIENTS

butter, for greasing

flour, for dusting

250 g/9 oz ready-made shortcrust pastry

1 tbsp olive oil

1 onion, roughly chopped

250 g/9 oz roasted red peppers in oil (drained weight), chopped

5 large eggs

½ tsp chopped fresh thyme

200 g/7 oz feta cheese (drained weight), chopped

freshly ground black pepper

SERVES 4–6

Roasted Red Pepper & Feta Tart

The warm flavours of the roasted peppers are perfectly complemented by the briny feta cheese.

METHOD

Preheat the oven to 220°C/425°F/Gas Mark 7. Grease a 23-cm/9 inch round flan tin.

Roll out the pastry on a work surface lightly dusted with flour to a round 5 cm/2 inches larger than the diameter of the tin. Use to line the tin, prick with a fork, line with baking paper and baking beans and bake in the preheated oven for 10 minutes. Remove the paper and beans and bake for a further 2 minutes.

Meanwhile, heat the oil in a frying pan over a medium heat, add the onion and cook until softened. Add the red peppers and cook until heated through.

Meanwhile, beat the eggs with the thyme and some pepper.

Remove the pastry case from the oven and reduce the oven temperature to 160°C/325°F/Gas Mark 3. Spread the onion and peppers mixture evenly over the base of the pastry case and scatter over the cheese. Pour in the egg mixture.

Return to the oven and bake for 30–35 minutes until the egg is set. Leave to cool for 5 minutes. Serve warm or cold.

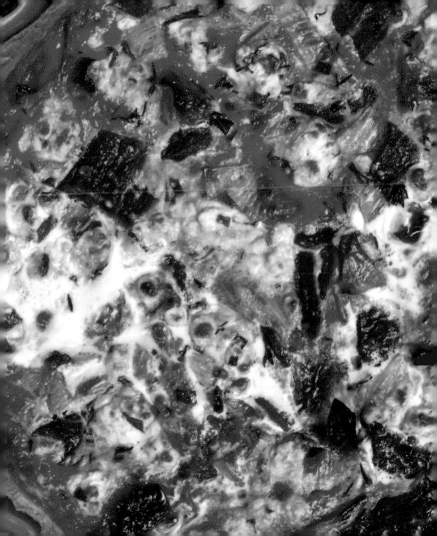

INGREDIENTS

4 tbsp olive oil
500 g/1 lb 2 oz
mixed wild
mushrooms, sliced
4 garlic cloves, finely
chopped
55 g/2 oz butter
1 onion, finely
chopped
350 g/12 oz
carnaroli or arborio
rice
50 ml/2 fl oz dry
white wine
1.2 litres/2 pints
simmering chicken
or vegetable stock
115 g/4 oz grated
Parmesan cheese
4 tbsp finely
chopped fresh
parsley
salt and freshly
ground black pepper

Wild Mushroom Risotto

If you can't get wild mushrooms, the
earthy flavour of chestnut mushrooms also
works very well in this dish.

METHOD

Heat 3 tablespoons of the oil in a frying pan. Add the
mushrooms and fry, stirring, for 2 minutes. Add the garlic and
cook, stirring, for 2 minutes. Transfer to a plate.

Heat the remaining oil and half the butter in a large saucepan.
Add the onion and cook, stirring, for 2 minutes until softened.

Reduce the heat, then add the rice and stir to coat in the oil and
butter. Add the wine and cook, stirring constantly, for 1 minute
until reduced.

Gradually add the simmering stock to the pan, a ladleful at a
time, stirring constantly. Wait until the previous ladleful has
been absorbed before adding the next. Cook for 20 minutes, or
until all the liquid has been absorbed and the rice is tender and
creamy.

Season to taste with salt and pepper, add the remaining butter
and the cheese and stir in the parsley. Serve immediately.

SERVES 4

INGREDIENTS

1 tbsp olive oil

2 tbsp seasoned flour

500 g/1 lb 2 oz neck of lamb, cut into large chunks

1 large onion, sliced

2 small carrots, sliced

300 ml/10 fl oz hot chicken or lamb stock

1 tbsp Worcestershire sauce

1 bay leaf

4 fresh thyme sprigs

600 g/1 lb 5 oz potatoes, thinly sliced

knob of butter

salt and freshly ground black pepper

Lamb Hotpot

This economical lamb dish is a great winter favourite. Serve with freshly cooked seasonal green vegetables.

METHOD

Preheat the oven to 190°C/375°F/Gas Mark 5. Heat the oil in a large, wide saucepan over a medium heat. Put the flour into a large bowl, add the lamb and toss to coat, then add the meat to the pan in batches and fry until browned all over. Remove from the pan and set aside.

Add the onion and carrots to the pan and cook for 5 minutes. Return the lamb to the pan and add the stock, Worcestershire sauce, bay leaf and thyme. Season to taste with salt and pepper and remove from the heat. Remove and discard the bay leaf and thyme sprigs.

Arrange half the potato slices in a shallow casserole dish in an overlapping layer. Top with the meat mixture, then layer the remaining potato slices on top and dot with the butter. Cover and cook in the preheated oven for 30 minutes, then remove the lid and cook for a further 20 minutes until the potatoes are golden brown.

SERVES 4

INGREDIENTS

1.7 kg/3 lb 10 oz
boned pork loin
1 tbsp olive oil
2 tbsp salt

Roast Pork Loin with Crackling

This makes a delicious winter Sunday roast. The secret of good crackling is to rub in lots of salt.

METHOD

Preheat the oven to 220°C/425°F/Gas Mark 7. Using a sharp knife, score the pork skin at 1-cm/½-inch intervals. Roll up the meat and tie with string to secure. Rub the skin with the oil and salt, and place the pork on a rack in a large roasting tin.

Roast in the preheated oven for 30 minutes, then reduce the oven temperature to 200°C/400°F/Gas Mark 6 and roast for a further 50 minutes–1 hour, or until the meat is cooked through and the skin is golden and crisp.

Remove from the oven and leave to stand for 10 minutes, then remove the string, slice the pork and serve with the crackling.

SERVES 4

INGREDIENTS

100 g/3½ oz stoned prunes

175 ml/6 fl oz beer

2 pork fillets, about 600 g/1 lb 5 oz total weight

1 tbsp olive oil

1 tbsp unsalted butter

2 shallots, finely chopped

2 tsp chopped fresh sage

salt and freshly ground black pepper

Pork Fillet Stuffed with Prunes

This is an unexpectedly delicious flavour combination. If you don't like prunes, try dried apricots instead.

METHOD

Put the prunes into a bowl with the beer and soak for 15–30 minutes. Drain, reserving the liquid, and set aside until needed.

Preheat the oven to 160°C/325°F/Gas Mark 3. Slit the fillets in half lengthways to make a pocket, then season the inside with salt and pepper. Place half the prunes in each fillet. Secure with wooden cocktail sticks.

Heat the oil and butter in a frying pan until hot. Add the fillets and cook for 3–4 minutes on each side, then transfer to an ovenproof dish. Sprinkle with 1–2 tablespoons of the reserved soaking liquid and bake in the preheated oven for 10–12 minutes.

Meanwhile, add the shallots to the pan and sauté for 3 minutes. Add the remaining soaking liquid and deglaze the pan for 2–3 minutes until the liquid is reduced by half. Add the sage and cook over a medium heat for about 5 minutes.

Take the meat out of the oven and remove the cocktail sticks. Transfer the fillets and all the cooking juices to the pan with the shallots and cook for a further 1–2 minutes, adding salt and pepper to taste.

Slice the fillets, then place on warmed serving plates. Pour over cooking juices and serve immediately.

SERVES 4-6

INGREDIENTS

500 g/1 lb 2 oz fresh chicken mince

1 egg, lightly beaten

2 garlic cloves, crushed

25 g/1 oz fresh white breadcrumbs

1 tbsp chopped fresh basil

1 tsp finely grated lemon rind

25 g/1 oz stoned black olives, chopped

25 g/1 oz Parmesan cheese, finely grated

40 g/1½ oz plain flour

2 tbsp olive oil

fresh basil sprigs, to garnish

classic green salad (see page 142), to serve

Lemon Parmigiana Chicken Rissoles

Parmesan cheese and lemon rind give these rissoles a delicious tang.

METHOD

Combine the chicken, egg, garlic, breadcrumbs, basil, lemon rind, olives and cheese in a bowl until the mixture comes together. Shape into eight equal-sized rissoles, no more than 2 cm/1¾ inches thick.

Spread the flour on a plate. Roll the rissoles in the flour until lightly coated. Place on a large plate, cover with clingfilm and chill in the refrigerator for 20 minutes.

Meanwhile, preheat the oven to 180°C/350°F/Gas Mark 4. Grease a large baking tray with a little oil.

Heat the remaining oil in a large frying pan over a medium heat. Add the rissoles, in batches if necessary, and cook for 1–2 minutes on each side, or until browned all over. Transfer to the prepared tray and bake in the preheated oven for 8–10 minutes, or until cooked through. Garnish with basil and serve with a green salad.

SERVES 4

INGREDIENTS

250 g/9 oz cooked ham

250 g/9 oz cooked turkey

2 tsp chopped fresh thyme

2 tsp chopped fresh sage

1 tbsp chopped fresh parsley

300 g/10½ oz mashed potatoes

3 shallots, chopped

1 large egg, lightly beaten

3 tbsp plain flour

2 tbsp olive oil

salt and white pepper

Zesty cranberry sauce

100 g/3½ oz soft light brown sugar

100 ml/3½ fl oz fresh orange juice

250 g/9 oz frozen cranberries

finely grated rind of 1 orange

SERVES 6

Turkey & Ham Rissoles with Zesty Cranberry Sauce

This is a very tasty way to use up all that leftover Christmas turkey and ham. The cranberry sauce is a delicious accompaniment.

METHOD

To make the sauce, put the sugar and orange juice into a saucepan and bring to the boil over a medium–high heat. Stir in the cranberries and orange rind, bring back to the boil, then reduce the heat and simmer for 5 minutes. Leave to cool and thicken, then store in the fridge for up to 1 week.

Place the ham and turkey in a food processor and process briefly until roughly chopped. Transfer to a large bowl, add the thyme, sage, parsley, potatoes, shallots and egg and mix to combine, seasoning with salt and pepper. Shape into 12 equal-sized rissoles, no more than 2 cm/1¾ inches thick.

Spread the flour on a plate and dip the rissoles in the flour, turning to coat completely. Heat the oil in a frying pan over a medium–high heat, add the rissoles in batches and fry for 1–2 minutes on each side, or until golden. Serve hot with the cranberry sauce.

INGREDIENTS

55 g/2 oz butter
550 g/1 lb 4 oz
chicken, cut into
small chunks
2 leeks, chopped
250 g/9 oz button
mushrooms, sliced
3 tbsp plain flour,
plus extra for dusting
300 ml/10 fl oz
chicken stock
150 ml/5 fl oz
double cream
3 tbsp dried tarragon
500 g/1 lb 2 oz
ready-made puff
pastry
1 egg, lightly
beaten, for glazing
salt and freshly
ground black pepper

Creamy Chicken Pie

This is the ultimate in comfort food. Leeks
and mushrooms, smothered in a creamy
tarragon sauce, bulk out the chicken.

METHOD

Preheat the oven to 190°C/375°F/Gas Mark 5. Melt half the
butter in a large frying pan over a medium–high heat, add the
chicken and fry until browned all over. Remove from the pan
and set aside.

Melt the remaining butter in the pan, add the leeks and
mushrooms and fry for 5 minutes, or until softened. Return the
chicken to the pan, sprinkle over the flour and stir well.

Add the stock, stirring, and season with salt and pepper. Reduce
the heat and simmer for 5 minutes. Remove from the heat, add
the cream, stirring well, then stir in the tarragon.

Roll out the pastry on a work surface lightly dusted with flour.
Place the chicken mixture in a pie dish and cover with the
pastry, trimming and crimping the edges. Brush with the egg,
pierce a couple of holes in the pastry to allow the steam to
escape during baking, then bake in the preheated oven for 30
minutes, or until the pastry is golden.

SERVES 4-6

INGREDIENTS

3 tbsp rapeseed oil
1 onion, chopped,
900 g/2 lb minced
lamb
2 carrots, chopped
2 tbsp finely
chopped fresh
parsley
1 tsp finely chopped
fresh thyme
1½ tbsp plain flour
700 ml/1¼ pints
lamb or beef stock
900 g/2 lb potatoes,
peeled and cut into
chunks
125 ml/4 fl oz milk
salt and freshly
ground black pepper

Shepherd's Pie

This is less common than cottage pie, which is made with beef, but it is a delicious way of using up the leftover Sunday lamb roast.

METHOD

Heat 2 tablespoons of the oil in a large frying pan over a medium heat. Add the onion and fry for 5 minutes until translucent. Add the lamb and cook, stirring, for 5 minutes until browned. Add the carrots, parsley and thyme and season with salt and pepper. Cook, stirring, for 2–3 minutes until the carrots are coated in oil.

Stir in the flour, then slowly pour in the stock and bring to the boil, scraping up any sediment from the base of the pan. Reduce the heat to low and simmer for 20–25 minutes until the sauce has thickened.

Meanwhile, preheat the oven to 200°C/400°F/Gas Mark 6. Put the potatoes into a large saucepan of lightly salted water, bring to the boil and cook for 10–12 minutes until tender. Drain and mash well with the milk.

Tip the pie filling into a large baking dish, cover with the potato and bake in the preheated oven for 30 minutes.

SERVES 4

INGREDIENTS

butter, for greasing
flour, for dusting
250 g/9 oz ready-made shortcrust pastry
225 g/8 oz baby spinach
3 tbsp olive oil
2 red onions, finely chopped
2 tbsp sugar
2 tbsp white wine
4 large eggs
350 ml/12 fl oz double cream
salt and freshly ground black pepper

SERVES 6

Caramelised Red Onion & Baby Spinach Tart

Sweet red onions lend themselves particularly well to being caramelised. The spinach makes a delicious and unexpected base for the tart.

METHOD

Preheat the oven to 180°C/350°F/Gas Mark 4. Grease a 23-cm/9-inch round tart tin with butter. Roll out the pastry on a work surface lightly dusted with flour, and use to line the prepared tin.

Put the spinach and 2 tablespoons of the oil into a food processor and process for 8 seconds until smooth.

Heat the remaining oil in a large frying pan over a medium heat. Add the onions and sugar and cook for 5–7 minutes, until the onions are beginning to caramelise. Stir in the wine and cook for 3–5 minutes, or until the wine has almost evaporated.

Put the eggs into a large bowl with the cream and beat for 3 minutes until blended. Season to taste with salt and pepper.

Spread the spinach mixture over the base of the pastry case and add a couple of torn leaves for colour. Top with the onions, making sure they are evenly distributed, then pour over the egg mixture. Bake in the preheated oven for 25–30 minutes, or until the filling is set. Leave to cool in the tin for 5 minutes, then serve warm.

INGREDIENTS

4 lamb's kidneys,
halved lengthways and
cored
1 tbsp olive oil
55 g/2 oz butter
1 onion, thinly sliced
1 fresh thyme sprig
1 tbsp sherry vinegar
1 tbsp sweet sherry
1 tsp tomato purée
1 pinch smoked hot
paprika
100 ml/3½ fl oz
double cream
2 slices sourdough
bread
1 tbsp sunflower oil
salt and freshly ground
black pepper
fresh parsley sprigs, to
garnish

Sherried Lamb's Kidneys on Fried Sourdough Bread

The sourdough bread makes this dish more substantial than it looks.

METHOD

Roughly chop the kidneys. Heat the olive oil and half the butter in a heavy-based frying pan over a medium heat, add the onion and thyme and fry until the onion is softened and translucent. Remove from the pan and set aside.

Increase the heat to high, add the kidneys to the pan with the remaining butter and fry, shaking the pan occasionally, for 3 minutes until coloured. Season to taste with salt and pepper.

Return the onion to the pan and pour in the vinegar and sherry stirring to deglaze the pan. Stir in the tomato purée, paprika and cream and cook for 1–2 minutes, stirring occasionally. If the sauce becomes too thick, add a little hot water to loosen it.

Meanwhile, trim the crusts from the bread and heat the sunflower oil in a separate frying pan until hot. Add the bread the pan and fry on both sides until golden and crisp.

Serve the kidneys on the bread, garnished with the parsley.

SERVES 2

INGREDIENTS

115 g/4 oz unsalted butter, plus extra for greasing

1 small onion, very finely chopped

25 g/1 oz fresh white breadcrumbs

finely grated zest and juice of 1 lemon

finely grated zest and juice of 1 lime

2 tsp chopped fresh tarragon, or 1 tsp dried tarragon

1 tsp ground coriander

250 g/9 oz ready-made puff pastry

4 salmon fillets, about 140 g/5 oz each

1 large egg, lightly beaten

boiled new potatoes and creamed spinach (see page 166), to serve

SERVES 4

Stuffed Salmon en Croûte

This impressive dish is extremely quick and easy to prepare. You can get ahead by preparing the filling in advance and assembling the pies at the last minute.

METHOD

Preheat the oven to 200°C/400°F/Gas Mark 6. Grease a large baking tray.

Melt the butter in a frying pan over a medium heat. Add the onion and cook for 3–5 minutes, until softened but not browned. Remove from the heat and stir in the breadcrumbs, lemon zest and juice, lime zest and juice, tarragon and coriander and mix well to combine.

Cut the pastry into four equal pieces, then roll out each piece to a 30 x 15-cm/12 x 6-inch rectangle. Place a salmon fillet on one half of each rectangle, leaving a 2.5-cm/1-inch border on three sides.

Place some of the onion mixture on each fillet, pressing down firmly to cover the fish. Brush the pastry borders with some of the egg, then fold over the pastry to make a parcel. Crimp the edges with a fork and prick the tops of the parcels once or twice to allow the steam to escape during baking. Brush with the beaten egg and place on the prepared tray.

Bake in the preheated oven for 30–35 minutes until golden. Serve hot, with new potatoes and creamed spinach.

INGREDIENTS

butter, for greasing

flour, for dusting

250 g/9 oz ready-made shortcrust pastry

5 large eggs

300 ml/10 fl oz single cream

½ tsp chopped fresh dill

250 g/9 oz smoked salmon trimmings, chopped

200 g/7 oz baby spinach, wilted

salt and freshly ground black pepper

fresh basil leaves, to garnish

Smoked Salmon Tart

Smoked salmon is usually eaten cold, but it is also delicious hot. This economical tart uses inexpensive smoked salmon trimmings.

METHOD

Preheat the oven to 200°C/400°F/Gas Mark 6. Grease a 23-cm/9-inch round flan tin.

Dust a work surface with flour and roll out the pastry to a round 5 cm/2 inches larger than the diameter of the tin. Use to line the tin, prick with a fork, then line with baking paper and baking beans and bake in the preheated oven for 10 minutes. Remove the paper and beans and bake for a further 2 minutes.

Meanwhile, beat the eggs with the cream, dill and a little salt and pepper, bearing in mind that smoked salmon is quite salty.

Remove the pastry case from the oven and reduce the oven temperature to 160°C/325°F/Gas Mark 3. Scatter the smoked salmon and the spinach evenly over the base of the pastry case, then pour in the egg mixture.

Return to the oven and bake for 30–35 minutes until the filling is set. Leave to cool for 5 minutes before serving, garnished with basil leaves.

SERVES 4-6

INGREDIENTS

75 g/2¾ oz butter
900 g/2 lb lobster
meat, cut into
2.5-cm/1-inch
chunks
125 ml/4 fl oz Irish
whiskey
175 ml/6 fl oz
double cream
1 tsp lemon juice
1 tsp wholegrain
mustard
salt and freshly
ground black pepper

Dublin Lawyer

This is an expensive dish, but very quick and easy to prepare. For a more economical version, use fresh crabmeat.

METHOD

Melt the butter in a saucepan over a low heat. Add the lobster and sauté until the meat is barely cooked through.

Remove the pan from the heat and pour in the whiskey. Carefully light it with a long grill lighter or a kitchen match. When the flames subside, return the pan to the heat and add the cream. Gradually stir in the mustard and lemon juice.

Increase the heat to medium and bring the mixture to the boil, then reduce the heat to low and add salt and pepper to taste.

Serve immediately on warmed plates with mashed potato and freshly cooked seasonal vegetables.

SERVES 4

INGREDIENTS

olive oil, for greasing
100 g/3½ oz butter, softened
1 tbsp chopped fresh parsley
1 tsp chopped fresh rosemary
4 trout fillets
salt and freshly ground black pepper
new potatoes and lemon wedges, to serve

Trout with Herb Butter

This is a lovely way to cook trout – the butter keeps the fish moist and the herbs are subtle enough not to overpower the delicate flavour of the trout.

METHOD

Preheat the oven to 200°C/400°F/Gas Mark 6. Line a baking tray with foil and grease the foil.

Put the butter into a bowl with the parsley and rosemary and mix well until combined. Season with salt and plenty of pepper.

Place the trout fillets on the prepared tray, skin side down, and spread with the parsley butter.

Bake in the preheated oven for 8–10 minutes, until the fish is opaque and just flaking.

Transfer the fish to warmed plates and serve immediately with new potatoes and lemon wedges.

SERVES 4

INGREDIENTS

650 g/1 lb 7 oz
white fish fillets,
skinned

250 g/9 oz cooked,
peeled prawns
(optional)

200 g/7 oz spinach,
cooked, drained and
finely chopped

55 g/2 oz butter,
plus extra for
greasing

1 onion, finely
chopped

150 ml/5 fl oz single
cream

1 tbsp English
mustard powder

juice of 1 lemon

1 kg/2 lb 4 oz
creamy mashed
potato

salt and freshly
ground black pepper

Luxury Fish Pie

Cod is the traditional ingredient in this
pie, but you could use any other white
fish. Prawns are not strictly necessary, but
add extra colour, flavour and texture.

METHOD

Preheat the oven to 180°C/350°F/Gas Mark 4. Grease a
2-litre/3½-pint baking dish.

Cut the fish into bite-sized pieces and place in the base of the
prepared dish. Scatter over the prawns and the spinach and
season to taste with salt and pepper.

Melt the butter in a saucepan, add the onion and fry over
a medium heat until softened. Add the cream and mustard
powder and slowly stir in the lemon juice. Bring to the boil,
stirring, then remove from the heat.

Pour the mixture into the dish, making sure that the fish and
prawns are evenly covered.

Pipe the mashed potato onto the fish mixture, then bake in th
preheated oven for 15–20 minutes, until the topping is golde
Serve hot.

SERVES 6

INGREDIENTS

butter, for greasing
450 g/1 lb cod
250 g/9 oz smoked haddock
175 g/6 oz salmon fillet
450 ml/16 fl oz fish stock
1 litre/1¾ pints milk
225 ml/8 fl oz dry white wine
2 tbsp cornflour
280 g/10 oz mature Cheddar cheese, coarsely grated
2 tbsp prepared English mustard
salt and freshly ground black pepper
fresh parsley sprigs, to garnish

Seafood Mornay

You can use any type of white fish for this and you could add some cooked prawns for extra flavour and texture.

METHOD

Preheat the oven to 200°C/400°F/Gas Mark 6. Grease a pie dish

Put the cod, haddock and salmon into a medium-sized frying pan. Add cold water to cover, then bring to a simmer over a medium heat and poach for 10 minutes. Drain, reserving the poaching liquid, and flake the fish with a fork. Transfer to the prepared pie dish.

Put the reserved liquid into a saucepan over a medium heat, ad the stock, 900 ml/1½ pints of the milk and the wine and bring the boil.

Whisk the remaining milk with the cornflour. Stir into the pan, reduce the heat and simmer, stirring, for 5 minutes, or until the sauce is beginning to thicken. Stir in half the cheese and the mustard and season to taste with salt and pepper.

Spoon the sauce over the fish and sprinkle over the remaining cheese. Bake in the preheated oven for 20–25 minutes until golden and bubbling. Serve hot, garnished with parsley sprigs.

SERVES 4

INGREDIENTS

4 x 175-g/6-oz
monkfish pieces

8 slices Parma ham

2 tbsp olive oil, plus
extra for greasing

fresh basil pesto, to
serve

cooked rice or roast
potatoes (see page
156), to serve

Monkfish Wrapped in Parma Har

This quick-to-prepare dish looks great – the
strong flavour of the fish is complemented
the ham and pesto.

METHOD

Preheat the oven to 180°C/350°F/Gas Mark 4. Grease a baking
dish.

Wrap each piece of fish in 2 slices of the ham. Heat the oil in a
large frying pan, add the fish parcels and cook for 2–3 minute
on each side.

Transfer to the prepared dish and roast in the preheated oven
for 10 minutes, or until the ham is beginning to crisp.

Serve on warmed plates with pesto and rice, or roast potatoes
you prefer.

SERVES 4

SIDES & SALADS

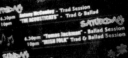

500 g/1 lb 2 oz
cooked chicken,
diced
1 celery stick, diced
4 spring onions,
trimmed and very
thinly sliced
1½ tsp chopped
fresh tarragon
2 tbsp chopped fresh
parsley
225 ml/8 fl oz
mayonnaise
2 tsp lemon juice
1 tsp wholegrain
mustard
2 tsp salt
freshly ground black
pepper, to taste
lettuce leaves,
tomato slices and
chopped avocado,
to serve

Chicken Salad

This is a good way to use leftover roast chicken, but it's so delicious you might find yourself cooking a chicken just to make the salad!

METHOD

Put the chicken, celery, spring onions, tarragon and parsley int a mixing bowl and toss to combine.

Put the mayonnaise, lemon juice, mustard, salt and pepper in small bowl and whisk to combine.

Add the dressing to the chicken mixture and stir gently until th chicken is coated in the dressing. Chill until ready to serve.

Serve on a bed of lettuce with some sliced tomato and choppe avocado, or use as a sandwich filling.

SERVES 4

INGREDIENTS

10 smoked bacon rashers, cut into small strips

2 tsp soft light brown sugar

125 ml/4 fl oz red wine vinegar

½ tsp prepared horseradish

¼ tsp freshly ground black pepper

10 spring onions, finely chopped

1 tbsp pine nuts

300 g/10½ oz baby lettuce leaves

Warm Bacon Salad with Pine Nuts

The crunchy smoked bacon dressing defines this salad. Use it on lettuce, spinach leaves or even diced potatoes.

METHOD

Put the bacon in a dry frying pan and fry until crisp. Crumble the bacon in the pan, then drain off all but 1 tablespoon of the bacon fat.

Add the sugar, vinegar, horseradish and pepper to the pan. Tip in the spring onions and sauté for 1 minute.

Toss the pine nuts in a separate dry frying pan for 1–2 minutes until toasted.

Pour the dressing over the lettuce leaves and toss to combine, then scatter over the pine nuts and serve.

SERVES 4-6

INGREDIENTS

75 g/2¾ oz
sunflower seeds
450 g/1 lb baby
spinach leaves
1 large apple, thinly
sliced
75 g/2¾ oz blue
cheese, crumbled

Dressing

2 tbsp cider vinegar
1 tsp honey
1 tbsp Dijon mustard
½ tsp salt
¼ tsp freshly ground
black pepper
3 tbsp extra virgin
olive oil
2 tbsp cold water
1 shallot, very finely
chopped

Baby Spinach Salad with Blue Cheese & Walnut Dressing

This is an unusual salad with lots of flavour, colour contrast and texture.

METHOD

To make the dressing, combine the vinegar, honey, mustard, salt and pepper in a small bowl. Whisk in the oil and water and stir in the shallot.

Put the sunflower seeds in a dry frying pan and toss over a medium heat for 5–6 minutes, until browned. Tip into a small bowl and leave to cool.

Toss the spinach leaves, apple, cheese and sunflower seeds with the dressing. Divide among six plates and serve immediately.

SERVES 6

INGREDIENTS

4 large handfuls mixed green salad leaves, rinsed and dried

3 tbsp extra virgin olive oil

1 tbsp white wine vinegar

salt and freshly ground black pepper

Classic Green Salad

Use the very freshest leaves when making this salad, and handle them gently so they don't bruise.

METHOD

Put the salad leaves in a large bowl.

Mix the oil, vinegar and salt and pepper to taste in a small bowl or put them into a lidded jar, cover and shake to combine.

Pour the dressing over the salad leaves and toss well to coat the leaves. Serve immediately.

SERVES 4

A Tale of Irish Cheesemaking

There is a long tradition of domestic cheesemaking in Ireland – references to cheesemaking in Irish literature date from as far back as the 12th century. Some believe that Irish missionary monks in Europe, including Saint Gall, returned to Ireland with the know-how to make cheese, and cheesemaking became prevalent in Irish monasteries. Others believe that Irish monks brought cheesemaking to Europe. Whatever its origins, cheesemaking was commonplace in medieval Ireland. Families produced cheese for their own use, made from sheep's, goat's or cow's milk, and cheese became central to their diet. By the end of the 18th century, however, the practice had died out – people needed to make and sell butter to survive, so there was no milk left over for cheesemaking, and they became almost completely reliant on potatoes as their staple diet.

In the 20th century there was renewed interest in cheesemaking, but this was initially focused on large-scale production of white and red Cheddar cheese for the Irish market and for export to the UK. For the most part, the cheese that was available to the general public was heavily processed. Then, in the 1970s, Irish people began to holiday in continental Europe.

where they encountered the wonderful variety of cheese produced by our European neighbours.

The long Irish domestic dairying tradition was revived in the 1970s and 1980s by owners and purchasers of smallholdings who became interested in producing their own cheese. These artisan cheeses, originally produced for the family, as in the past, gradually began to be sold locally and served in local restaurants, eventually achieving a national and then international reputation. All of the cheeses are individual, produced from the milk of pasture-fed animals, so the flavours are particular to an area, or even to a farm. Cheese production is still individual, with different farms producing different cheeses to their own recipes, using their own milk – and that is what makes them so special.

INGREDIENTS

1 small red onion, thinly sliced

1 large cos lettuce, torn into bite-sized pieces

12 cherry tomatoes, halved

1 cucumber, thinly sliced

Dressing

1 tbsp red wine vinegar

2 tbsp balsamic vinegar

1 tbsp Dijon mustard

1 tsp soft light brown sugar

1 garlic clove, crushed

175 ml/6 fl oz extra virgin olive oil

salt and freshly ground black pepper

Mixed Salad

A colourful classic salad that is excellent with grilled meat and savoury tarts.

METHOD

Put the onion, lettuce, tomatoes and cucumber into a large bowl.

To make the dressing, put the red wine vinegar, balsamic vinegar, mustard, sugar and garlic into a small bowl and whisk to combine. Slowly whisk in the oil until smooth. Season to taste with salt and pepper.

Pour the dressing over the salad ingredients and toss well to coat. Serve immediately.

SERVES 4

INGREDIENTS

200 ml/7 fl oz milk
6 spring onions, trimmed and finely chopped
450 g/1 lb shredded green cabbage
450 g/1 lb potatoes, peeled, cooked, drained and mashed
55 g/2 oz butter
salt and freshly ground black pepper

Colcannon

This is similar to the British bubble and squeak, but this dish is cooked from scratch, not with leftovers.

METHOD

Put the milk into a saucepan, add the spring onions and cook over a low heat for 5 minutes.

Bring a saucepan of lightly salted water to the boil, add the cabbage, bring back to the boil and cook for 5 minutes, until just tender. Drain and add to the potatoes, mixing to combine.

Add the spring onion and milk mixture and half the butter. Beat the mixture, season well and serve with the remaining butter dotted on top.

SERVES 4

INGREDIENTS

250 g/9 oz raw
potatoes, peeled
250 g/9 oz mashed
potatoes
250 g/9 oz plain
flour
good pinch of
bicarbonate of soda
pinch of salt
225 ml/8 fl oz
buttermilk, plus extra
if needed
butter, for frying
chopped fresh dill, to
garnish

Boxty

This substantial savoury pancake is made with raw and cooked potatoes and cooked in butter.

METHOD

Grate the raw potatoes into a colander lined with kitchen paper. Press another sheet of paper on top and squeeze out as much liquid as possible. Mix with the mashed potatoes.

Add the flour, bicarbonate of soda and salt. Mix in enough buttermilk to make a soft batter.

Preheat a large, heavy-based frying pan or griddle pan, melt the butter, then drop in large spoonfuls of the batter. Cook over a medium heat for 3 minutes on each side until golden. Garnish with dill and serve immediately on warmed plates.

SERVES 4

INGREDIENTS

450 g/1 lb baby new potatoes, halved

6 tbsp lemon juice, or to taste

4 tbsp extra virgin olive oil

1 small cucumber, chopped

1 celery stick, finely chopped

4 spring onions, sliced

3 tbsp chopped fresh parsley

3 tbsp chopped fresh mint

salt and freshly ground black pepper

New Potato Salad with Mint

New potatoes go very well with mint. This is very good with poached salmon.

METHOD

Cook the potatoes in boiling water until just tender, then drain dry and cut in half.

Mix the lemon juice and oil with salt and pepper to taste in a large salad bowl. Add the cucumber, celery, spring onions, parsley, mint and potatoes and mix well, making sure that the mint and parsley are well distributed. Serve immediately.

SERVES 4

INGREDIENTS

butter, for frying
500 g/1 lb 2 oz
boiled unpeeled
potatoes, cut into
1-cm/½-inch slices
salt and freshly
ground black pepper
fresh rosemary
sprigs, to garnish

Crunchy Fried Potatoes

Leaving the skins on gives the potatoes a lovely crunch. These are often included in a full Irish breakfast.

METHOD

Melt enough butter for frying in a large, heavy-based frying pan.

Add the potatoes in a single layer, season to taste with salt and pepper and fry, without turning, over a medium heat until golden, then turn and cook on the other side.

Transfer to a warmed dish, garnish with rosemary and serve immediately.

SERVES 4

INGREDIENTS

125 ml/4 fl oz
vegetable oil, olive
oil, duck fat or goose
fat
1.5 kg/3 lb 5 oz
potatoes, peeled and
quartered
1 tbsp plain flour
salt

Roast Potatoes

A great accompaniment to any roast meat,
these will be even more delicious if you
use goose or duck fat instead of oil.

METHOD

Preheat the oven to 200°C/400°F/Gas Mark 6. Pour the oil into
large roasting tin and place in the oven to heat.

Bring a large saucepan of lightly salted water to the boil, add
the potatoes, bring back to the boil and cook for 5 minutes.
Remove from the heat and drain in a colander, shaking the
potatoes backwards and forwards to fluff up the edges.

Sprinkle the potatoes with the flour and shake until thinly
coated.

Carefully add the potatoes to the tin and roll them to coat in
the oil. Spread them in the tin in a single layer and roast for
15 minutes. Turn and roast for a further 15 minutes, then turn
again and roast for a further 15 minutes, or until golden and
crisp all over.

Transfer to a warmed dish, season with a little salt and serve
immediately.

SERVES 6

INGREDIENTS

butter, for greasing
6 potatoes, sliced
1 onion, thinly sliced
225 g/8 oz Cheddar
cheese, grated
2 garlic cloves,
crushed
250 ml/9 fl oz single
cream
chopped fresh
parsley, to garnish

Cheesy Potatoes with Garlic & Cream

This rich dish is a good accompaniment to grilled chicken and roast meat. Serve with bacon for lunch.

METHOD

Preheat the oven to 180°C/350°F/Gas Mark 4. Grease a large casserole dish.

Layer the potato slices in the prepared dish, alternating with slices of onion. Sprinkle over the cheese.

Mix the garlic with the cream and pour over the potatoes. Cover and bake in the preheated oven for 1 hour, or until the potatoes are tender.

Uncover and bake for a further 15–20 minutes until the top is golden brown. Leave to stand for 15 minutes before serving, garnished with parsley.

SERVES 4–6

INGREDIENTS

4 large baking
potatoes

Jacket Potatoes and Toppings

Potatoes baked in their skins are great
with stews and casseroles. With our simple
toppings, they're a meal in themselves.

METHOD

Preheat the oven to 180°C/325°F/Gas Mark 4. Prick the potatoes
several times with a fork and place on a shelf in the hottest part
of the oven. Bake for approximately 1 hour, or until soft inside.
Remove from the oven, cut a slot or cross into each potato so
that you can pull it apart slightly.

To make the toppings, mix the ingredients together. Serve with
the potatoes.

Cheese & onion topping

100 g/3½ oz mozzarella
cheese, grated
100 g/3½ oz mature
Cheddar cheese, grated
4 spring onions, finely
sliced
3 tbsp milk
pinch of freshly ground
black pepper

Spicy tuna & cottage cheese topping

225 g/8 oz canned tuna in brine
(drained weight)
½ red chilli, finely chopped
1 spring onion, finely chopped
6 cherry tomatoes, halved
1 tbsp chopped fresh parsley or
coriander
150 g/5½ oz cottage cheese

Paprika bean topping

1 tbsp sunflower oil
1 carrot, diced
1 celery stick, diced
400 g/14 oz canned haricot
beans, drained
2 tomatoes, chopped
1 tsp paprika
1 tsp Worcestershire sauce

SERVES 4-6

450 g/1 lb shelled
garden peas
1 tsp sugar
1 fresh mint sprig
25 g/1 oz butter
salt
fresh mint leaves, to
garnish

Minted Peas

Nothing says 'summer' quite like peas fresh from the garden. Cooking and serving them with a little mint really brings out their sweet flavour.

METHOD

Bring a saucepan of lightly salted water to the boil, add the peas, sugar and mint sprig, bring back to the boil and cook for about 4 minutes until just tender.

Drain, toss with the butter and transfer to a warmed serving dish. Garnish with mint leaves and serve immediately.

SERVES 6–8

INGREDIENTS

500 g/1 lb 2 oz
baby carrots, washed
but not peeled

2 tsp sugar

55 g/2 oz butter

salt and freshly
ground black pepper

chopped fresh dill, to
garnish

Baby Carrots with Dill

These new season carrots, with their swee
and glossy coating, are the perfect partner
for roast lamb or chicken.

METHOD

Put the whole carrots into a saucepan with just enough water to
cover, then add the sugar and butter.

Bring to the boil, then reduce the heat and simmer until the
water has evaporated and the carrots are tender.

Transfer to a warmed serving dish, season to taste with salt and
pepper, garnish with dill and serve immediately.

SERVES 4

INGREDIENTS

25 g/1 oz butter
1 small onion, finely chopped
2 tbsp plain flour
200 ml/7 fl oz milk
400 g/14 oz spinach
100 ml/3½ fl oz single cream
salt and freshly ground black pepper

Creamed Spinach

A deliciously easy way to prepare spinach – this is perfect for serving with the Sunda roast or a baked ham.

METHOD

Heat the butter in a saucepan, then add the onion and cook for 5 minutes until softened. Stir in the flour and cook for a further 2 minutes, then gradually whisk in the milk until it has all been incorporated. Cook for 5 minutes until the sauce has thickened

Meanwhile, put the spinach into a large colander. Pour over boiling water until the leaves have wilted. Place the spinach in a clean tea towel, squeeze out any excess liquid, then roughly chop.

Stir the spinach into the sauce with the cream, heat over a low heat, then season to taste with salt and pepper and serve.

SERVES 6-8

INGREDIENTS

1 head of red cabbage

1 cooking apple, peeled, cored and roughly chopped

1 red onion, finely chopped

1 tbsp soft light brown sugar

large pinch of mixed spice

½ tsp ground cloves

½ tsp freshly ground nutmeg

150 ml/5 fl oz red wine vinegar

knob of butter

Spiced Red Cabbage

This cabbage is perfect with any pork, ham or bacon dish. The long slow cooking will fill your home with the wonderful aroma of spices.

METHOD

Preheat the oven to 150°C/300°F/Gas Mark 2.

Remove the tough outer leaves of the cabbage, then cut it into quarters and use a sharp knife to cut out the core. Thinly slice the quarters vertically and place in a large casserole dish.

Add the apple, onion, sugar and spices and pour over the vinegar. Mix well together.

Cover tightly and cook in the preheated oven for 2–3 hours, uncovering and stirring occasionally. Add the butter 30 minutes before the end of cooking and stir to combine.

Remove from the oven, transfer to a warmed serving dish and leave to cool a little before serving.

SERVES 4-6

INGREDIENTS

450 g/1 lb kale, stems and central ribs removed

3 tbsp butter, plus extra to serve

3 tbsp fresh lemon juice

3 tbsp balsamic vinegar

salt and freshly ground black pepper

Kale with Lemon & Butter

This often-overlooked green leaf is a good source of fibre, iron, calcium and antioxidants. It's delicious when cooked with lemon.

METHOD

Bring a large saucepan of water to the boil. Add the kale, bring back to the boil and cook for 3 minutes. Drain very well and transfer to a serving dish.

Meanwhile, melt the butter in a frying pan over a medium–high heat. Add the lemon juice and vinegar and season to taste with salt and pepper. Cook for 30 seconds, stirring with a whisk.

Pour the butter mixture over the kale, toss to coat and serve immediately with a knob of butter on top.

SERVES 4

INGREDIENTS

8 small onions
4 fresh thyme sprigs
350 ml/12 fl oz
double cream
salt and freshly
ground black pepper

Creamy Onion Bake

This rich dish raises the humble onion to the realms of gourmet food. Serve with roast meat or chicken.

METHOD

Preheat the oven to 180°C/350°F/Gas Mark 4. Bring a large saucepan of lightly salted water to the boil. Add the whole peeled onions, bring back to the boil and bubble for about 20 minutes, until tender.

Remove from the heat and drain. Cut the onions in half vertically and place them in a single layer in a baking dish. Scatter over the thyme, pour in the cream and season to taste with salt and pepper.

Bake in the preheated oven for 20–25 minutes until bubbling.

Remove the thyme sprigs and serve straight from the dish.

SERVES 4

INGREDIENTS

2 kg/4 lb 8 oz floury
potatoes, cut into
chunks

15 spring onions,
roughly chopped

400 ml/14 fl oz milk

115 g/4 oz butter,
melted

salt and freshly
ground black pepper

Champ

A classic Halloween dish, this was
traditionally made with nettle tips, but
now we usually use chives or spring
onions.

METHOD

Bring the potatoes to the boil in a large saucepan of water, then
cook for 20 minutes until tender. Drain and set aside.

Meanwhile, put the spring onions into a saucepan with the
milk, bring to the boil, then simmer for 5 minutes. Drain the
spring onions, reserving the milk.

Mash the potatoes with the milk until smooth and creamy. Stir
in the spring onions and season to taste with salt and pepper.

Transfer to a serving dish and make a well in the centre. Pour
the butter into the well and serve immediately.

SERVES 4

INGREDIENTS

4 large parsnips, peeled and cut into thick sticks
1 tbsp olive oil
2 garlic cloves, finely chopped
1 tbsp clear honey
1 tsp chopped fresh sage
chopped fresh parsley, to garnish

Roast Parsnips

Parsnips are very sweet when roasted and are delicious with roast meat of any kind. Here they're basted with oil and honey and roasted with a little sage.

METHOD

Preheat the oven to 230°C/450°F/Gas Mark 8.

Put the parsnips in a large bowl, add the oil, garlic, honey and sage and toss to coat.

Reserving the liquid in the bowl, place the parsnips in a baking dish in a single layer and roast in the preheated oven for 30 minutes until tender. Remove from the oven, toss with the reserved liquid, garnish with parsley and serve immediately.

SERVES 4

INGREDIENTS

6 large leeks,
trimmed

3½ tbsp olive oil

1 tsp chopped fresh
thyme

salt and freshly
ground black pepper

thyme sprigs, to
garnish

lemon wedges, to
serve

Baked Leeks

Leeks grow well in Ireland and are a
simple but delicious accompaniment to a
variety of dishes, including roast meat.

METHOD

Preheat the oven to 230°C/450°F/Gas Mark 8. Cut the leeks in
half lengthways, then arrange them in the base of a baking dish
in a single layer.

Brush all over with the oil, then season to taste with salt and
pepper and sprinkle over the thyme.

Bake in the preheated oven for 20–25 minutes, turning once,
until the leeks are beginning to blacken around the edges.
Serve immediately, with thyme sprigs and lemon wedges for
squeezing over.

SERVES 6

DESSERTS

INGREDIENTS

butter, for greasing

plain flour, for dusting

250 g/9 oz ready-made shortcrust pastry

150 g/5½ oz plain chocolate (at least 70% cocoa solids)

2 eggs, beaten

1 tbsp single cream

2 large ripe pears

1 tbsp caster sugar

fresh mint leaves, to decorate

whipped cream, to serve

SERVES 6

Pear & Chocolate Tart

This impressive tart is deceptively simple to make – because the pears are sliced so thinly, they need no pre-cooking.

METHOD

Preheat the oven to 180°C/350°F/Gas Mark 4. Grease a 20-cm/8 inch round loose-based tart tin.

Roll out the pastry on a work surface lightly dusted with flour t a round 5 cm/2 inches larger than the diameter of the tin. Use to line the tart tin. Prick with a fork, line with baking paper and fill with baking beans, then bake in the preheated oven for 15 minutes. Remove from the oven, take out the paper and beans, and increase the oven temperature to 190°C/375°F/Gas Mark 5

Put the chocolate into a bowl set over a saucepan of gently simmering water and heat until melted. Remove from the heat and leave to cool slightly, then beat in the eggs. Fold in the cream. Spread the chocolate mixture evenly over the base of th pastry case.

Peel and core the pears and cut them lengthways into thin slices. Arrange the pear slices on the chocolate in an overlapping pattern and sprinkle over the caster sugar.

Bake for about 25 minutes until the pears are golden brown. Leave to cool completely, garnish with mint and serve with whipped cream.

INGREDIENTS

butter, for greasing

flour, for dusting

250 g/9 oz
ready-made sweet
shortcrust pastry

400 ml/14 fl oz
double cream

140 g/5 oz plain
chocolate, roughly
chopped

2 tbsp whiskey

2 tbsp icing sugar

Chocolate Whiskey Mousse Tart

A rich tart that should be served after
a light meal – the whiskey is just a
suggestion.

METHOD

Preheat the oven to 200°C/400°F/Gas Mark 6. Grease a 23-cm/
9-inch round tart tin.

Roll out the pastry on a work surface lightly dusted with flour
to a round 5 cm/2 inches larger than the diameter of the tin.
Use to line the tin. Prick with a fork, line with baking paper and
fill with baking beans, then bake in the preheated oven for 10
minutes. Remove the paper and beans and bake for a further
2 minutes, then leave to cool in the tin.

Meanwhile, put 175 ml/6 fl oz of the cream in a saucepan and
bring to a simmer over a low heat. Remove from the heat and
add the chocolate, stirring until melted and combined. Leave to
cool to room temperature, then stir in the whiskey.

Whip the remaining cream with the icing sugar until stiff peaks
form. Gently fold in the chocolate mixture until combined.

Pour the chocolate filling into the pastry case and chill for 1
hour 30 minutes, or until set. Serve chilled. It will keep in the
fridge for up to 2 days.

SERVES 8–10

INGREDIENTS

85 g/3 oz butter, melted

225 g/8 oz digestive biscuit crumbs

700 g/1 lb 9 oz cream cheese, softened

115 g/4 oz sugar

3 eggs, beaten

2 tbsp plain flour

225 ml/8 fl oz Irish cream liqueur

1 tsp vanilla extract

ready-made strawberry sauce and fresh mint leaves, to decorate

Irish Cream Cheesecake

This plain baked cheesecake is given a touch of creamy luxury with the addition of a healthy glug of Irish cream liqueur.

METHOD

Preheat the oven to 180°C/350°F/Gas Mark 4. Mix the butter and biscuit crumbs together and press into the base of a 20-cm/8-inch round springform cake tin. Bake in the preheated oven for 5 minutes. Remove from the oven (do not switch off the oven).

Meanwhile, put the cheese and sugar into a bowl and mix to combine, then add the eggs, flour, liqueur and vanilla extract and beat until smooth.

Pour the mixture onto the crumb base, return to the oven and bake for 40 minutes. Leave to cool, then chill overnight. When ready to serve, release and remove the springform and transfer the cheesecake to a serving plate, drizzle over some strawberry sauce and decorate with mint leaves.

SERVES 8-10

INGREDIENTS

250 g/9 oz digestive
biscuits
125 g/4½ oz
butter, plus extra for
greasing
3 tsp powdered
gelatine
4 tbsp boiling water
500 g/1 lb 2 oz
cream cheese,
softened
100 g/3½ oz caster
sugar
1 tsp vanilla bean
paste
300 ml/10 fl oz
whipping cream
300 g/10½ oz frozen
blueberries
icing sugar, for
dusting

Blueberry Cheesecake

Cheesecake is one of Ireland's favourite
desserts – this luscious no-bake version
with blueberries is a classic.

METHOD

Grease a 20-cm/8-inch round springform cake tin. Put the
biscuits into a food processor and process until coarse crumbs
form. Add the butter and pulse to combine. Press the mixture
into the base and up the side of the prepared tin. Chill for 20
minutes until firm.

Meanwhile, sprinkle the gelatine over the boiling water,
whisking with a fork until dissolved. Leave to cool for 15
minutes.

Beat the cheese, sugar and vanilla bean paste together until
smooth. Whip the cream until soft peaks form, then fold
into the cheese mixture. Stir in the blueberries (they will
immediately begin to leak colour into the mixture) and pour
the mixture into the tin.

Cover and chill for at least 8 hours, then release and remove
the springform and transfer the cheesecake to a plate. Dust with
icing sugar and serve.

SERVES 6–8

INGREDIENTS

butter, for greasing
100 g/3½ oz plain chocolate
4 eggs, separated
100 g/3½ oz caster sugar, plus extra for sprinkling
a mixture of icing sugar and cocoa powder, to decorate

Filling

300 ml/10 fl oz double cream
2 tbsp icing sugar
225 g/8 oz fresh raspberries

Raspberry & Chocolate Roulade

This is a great dessert for a party – it looks spectacular and will go a long way. The rolling isn't as difficult as you might think.

METHOD

Preheat the oven to 180°C/350°F/Gas Mark 4. Grease and line a 23 x 3 cm/9 x 13-inch Swiss roll tin.

Place the chocolate in a heatproof bowl set over a saucepan of gently simmering water and heat until melted. Place the egg whites in a large grease-free bowl and whisk until soft peaks form. Set aside.

Place the egg yolks and sugar in a large heatproof bowl set over a saucepan of simmering water. Whisk until the mixture is fluffy and thi enough to leave a trail when the whisk is lifted from the mixture. Stir the chocolate, then gently fold in the egg whites. Pour into the prepar tin and bake in the preheated oven for 20–25 minutes, or until the centre of the cake springs back when lightly touched with your finger.

Meanwhile, lay a sheet of baking paper on the work surface and sprin with a little caster sugar. Turn out the roulade onto the paper, then carefully peel away the lining paper. Trim the edges and cover the roulade with a damp tea towel. Leave to cool.

Whip the cream with the icing sugar until soft peaks form, then gently fold in half the raspberries. Spread the cream mixture over the roulad and scatter over the remaining raspberries. Starting from one of the narrow ends, carefully roll up the roulade using the paper to help – don't worry if it cracks a little. Transfer to a serving plate, dust with th icing sugar and cocoa mixture and serve.

SERVES 12

INGREDIENTS

Pâte sucré

150 g/5½ oz plain flour, plus extra for dusting

pinch of salt

75 g/2¾ oz unsalted butter, plus extra for greasing

55 g/2 oz icing sugar

2 large egg yolks

Filling

1 large egg

4 large egg yolks

150 g/5½ oz caster sugar

finely grated zest and juice of 4 lemons

150 ml/5 fl oz double cream

lemon slices, to decorate

SERVES 8

Lemon Tart

This creamy yet zesty baked tart is the perfect finishing touch to a big meal.

METHOD

To make the pâte sucré, put the flour, salt and butter into a food processor and pulse until fine crumbs form. Add the sugar and pulse, then add the egg yolks and pulse again until the mixture comes together loosely. Turn out the dough onto a work surface lightly dusted with flour. Knead to bring the mixture together, then shape into a ball and flatten slightly. Wrap in clingfilm, then chill for at least 30 minutes.

Grease a 23-cm/9-inch loose-based tart tin. Roll out the pâte sucré on a work surface lightly dusted with flour to a round 2.5 cm/1 inch larger than the diameter of the tin. Use to line the tin and chill for 30 minutes.

Meanwhile preheat the oven to 190°C/375°F/Gas Mark 5. Prick the base of the pastry case, line with baking paper and fill with baking beans, then bake in the preheated oven for 10 minutes. Remove the paper and beans, return to the oven and bake for 8–10 minutes. Reduce the oven temperature to 160°C/325°F/Gas Mark 3.

To make the filling, put the egg yolks and sugar into a bowl and beat until smooth. Stir in the lemon zest and juice and the cream and mix to combine.

Put the tin in the oven, carefully pour in the filling and bake for 25–30 minutes. Leave to cool for 15 minutes, then serve warm, or leave to cool completely and chill until ready to serve. Decorate with lemon slices.

INGREDIENTS

225 g/8 oz butter
1 kg/2 lb 4 oz
Bramley apples,
peeled, cored and
thinly sliced
115 g/4 oz sugar
1 tbsp lemon juice
grated rind of 1
lemon
2 egg yolks, beaten
10 slices of day-old
white bread, crusts
removed
whipped cream, to
serve

Apple Charlotte

A delicious dessert that makes good use o
day-old bread. It's a little fiddly to prepar
but the result is spectacular.

METHOD

Preheat the oven to 200°C/400°F/Gas Mark 6. Melt half the butter in a
large, heavy-based saucepan over a medium heat. Add the apples, sug
lemon juice, lemon rind and about 3 tablespoons of water.

Bring to the boil slowly, then reduce the heat, cover and cook for abo
20–25 minutes until the apples are soft. Uncover, increase the heat to
high and cook vigorously for 5 minutes.

Remove from the heat and stir in the egg yolks. Melt the remaining
butter and use some of it to brush the sides and base of a 23-cm/9-inc
Charlotte mould or round springform cake tin. Line the base with
baking paper.

Cut the bread into strips 3 cm/1¼ inches wide and as tall as the tin. D
the strips in the remaining melted butter and arrange over the base a
around the side of the tin, reserving some for the top. Spoon in the
apple mixture, then place the remaining bread on top.

Bake in the preheated oven for 20 minutes, then reduce the oven
temperature to 190°C/375°F/Gas Mark 5 and bake for a further 35
minutes, until the top is a deep golden brown.

Leave to cool in the tin for 15 minutes, then carefully turn out of the
mould. Serve warm or cold, with whipped cream.

SERVES 6

INGREDIENTS

300 g/10½ oz
ready-made
shortcrust pastry

plain flour, for
dusting

150 g/5½ oz golden
caster sugar, plus
extra for dusting

½ tsp cinnamon

1 kg/2 lb 4 oz
Bramley apples,
cored, peeled and
thickly sliced

1 egg white, beaten,
for brushing

whipped cream or
vanilla ice cream, to
serve

Apple Pie with Cream

Apple pie is the ultimate in comfort food.
This one is full of succulent Bramley
apples and is delicious served with lots of
whipped cream.

METHOD

Preheat the oven to 190°C/375°F/Gas Mark 5. Cut off a third of
the pastry and set aside until needed. Roll out the remaining
pastry on a work surface lightly dusted with flour and use to
line a deep 20-cm/8-inch pie tin, leaving an overhang. If you
prefer, you can make a lattice crust as an attractive alternative.

Mix the sugar and cinnamon together in a large bowl, then toss
the apples in the mixture. Put the apples into the pie tin.

Roll out the reserved pastry to a round about 2.5 cm/1 inch
larger than the diameter of the top of the tin. Brush some cold
water around the pastry rim, then lay the pastry round on top,
crimping the edges to seal. Pierce the pastry about five times to
allow the steam to escape during baking.

Brush the pie with the egg white and dust with sugar. Bake in
the preheated oven for 40–45 minutes until golden. Dust with
more sugar, then serve with whipped cream or ice cream.

SERVES 8

INGREDIENTS

butter, for greasing

plain flour, for dusting

250 g/9 oz ready-made shortcrust pastry

150 g/5 oz fresh white breadcrumbs

225 ml/8 fl oz golden syrup

1 egg, beaten, for brushing

golden caster sugar, for sprinkling

whipped cream or vanilla ice cream, to serve

Golden Syrup Tart

Golden syrup has been a staple pantry ingredient in Ireland for more than 50 years, so it's easy to make this delicious tart at short notice.

METHOD

Preheat the oven to 180°C/350°F/Gas Mark 4. Grease a 20-cm/8-inch loose-based tart tin.

Roll out the pastry on a work surface lightly dusted with flour and use to line the prepared tin.

Mix the breadcrumbs and golden syrup together and spread evenly in the pastry case.

Re-roll the pastry trimmings and cut out several 5-mm/¼-inch wide strips, slightly longer than the diameter of the tin. Weave the pastry strips into a lattice pattern over the top of the tart, pressing the ends into the edge of the pastry case.

Bake in the preheated oven for 20 minutes. Brush the pastry with the beaten egg and sprinkle the tart with sugar, then return to the oven for a further 15 minutes, or until the pastry is golden.

Leave to cool for 15–20 minutes, then cut into wedges and serve with whipped cream or ice cream.

SERVES 6-8

INGREDIENTS

450 g/1 lb trimmed rhubarb, cut into 2.5-cm/1-inch lengths

100 g/3½ oz caster sugar

1 tsp grated fresh ginger

150 g/5½ oz self-raising flour

85 g/3 oz butter, at room temperature

55 g/2 oz demerara sugar

55 g/2 oz hazelnuts, finely chopped

custard (see page 212), to serve

Rhubarb & Ginger Crumble

Don't be tempted to replace the fresh ginger with ground ginger – it's the fresh root that gives this dessert its depth of spicy flavour.

METHOD

Put the rhubarb into a saucepan with the caster sugar, ginger and 2–3 tablespoons of water. Cook over a low heat for about 15 minutes until it is just bubbling, and the rhubarb is soft but not disintegrating. Transfer to a baking dish.

Meanwhile, preheat the oven to 200°C/400°F/Gas Mark 6. Sift the flour into a bowl, cut in the butter and mix with your fingertips until soft and crumbly.

Add the sugar and nuts and mix to combine, then sprinkle the crumble over the rhubarb.

Bake in the preheated oven for 30 minutes, then serve hot, with lots of custard.

SERVES 6

INGREDIENTS

6 thin slices of white bread, crusts removed

55 g/2 oz butter, plus extra for greasing

55 g/2 oz currants

55 g/2 oz sultanas

55 g/2 oz caster sugar

2 eggs

300 ml/10 fl oz milk

300 ml/10 fl oz single cream

custard (see page 212), to serve

Luxury Bread & Butter Pudding

A lovely, filling dessert that oozes comfort – this luxurious version is prepared with milk and cream.

METHOD

Spread the bread with the butter and cut into triangles. Grease a 1-litre/1¾-pint ovenproof dish and arrange half the bread triangles in the base. Sprinkle with the currants, sultanas and half the sugar.

Top with the remaining bread, buttered side up, and sprinkle with the remaining sugar.

Beat the eggs, milk and cream together and pour over the bread. Leave to stand for 30 minutes.

Meanwhile, preheat the oven to 160°C/325°F/Gas Mark 3. Bake the pudding for 45–60 minutes until set and browned on top.

Serve hot, with custard.

SERVES 4

INGREDIENTS

250 g/9 oz digestive
biscuits
125 g/4½ oz
butter, plus extra for
greasing
4 small bananas
300 ml/10 fl oz
whipping cream,
lightly whipped
cocoa powder or
grated chocolate, to
decorate

Filling
100 g/3½ oz butter
100 g/3½ oz soft
dark brown sugar
400 ml/14 fl oz
canned condensed
milk

Banoffee Pie

This lusciously indulgent dessert is always
a big hit with children (and most adults!).
A little goes a long way.

METHOD

Grease a 20-cm/8-inch round springform cake tin. Put the
biscuits into a food processor and process until coarse crumbs
form. Add the butter and pulse to combine. Press the mixture
into the base and up the side of the prepared tin. Chill for 20
minutes until firm.

To make the filling, put the butter and sugar into a saucepan
and heat, stirring constantly, until the butter has melted and
the sugar is dissolved. Add the condensed milk, bring to the
boil and boil rapidly for 1–2 minutes, stirring constantly, until a
thick caramel forms. Spread over the biscuit base, leave to cool,
then chill for at least 1 hour until firm.

When ready to serve, release and remove the springform and
place the pie on a serving plate. Slice the bananas and fold
them into the cream, then spoon the mixture over the caramel.
Decorate with cocoa powder or grated chocolate and serve
immediately.

SERVES 8

INGREDIENTS

4 egg whites
250 g/9 oz caster
sugar
1 tsp white wine
vinegar
1 tsp cornflour
½ tsp vanilla extract
700 g/1 lb 9 oz
strawberries, hulled
and halved
3 tbsp icing sugar
350 ml/12 fl oz
double cream

Pavlova

This light and delicious dessert is a great way of using up leftover egg whites. You can use any fresh soft fruit.

METHOD

Preheat the oven to 150°C/300°F/Gas Mark 2. Draw a 23-cm/ 9-inch circle on a piece of baking paper.

Whisk the egg whites until stiff peaks form, then gradually whisk in the caster sugar until the mixture is glossy. Whisk in the vinegar, cornflour and vanilla extract.

Spread the meringue inside the circle drawn on the baking paper, making the sides higher than the centre. Bake in the preheated oven for 1 hour, then switch off the oven and leave the meringue inside to cool completely.

To make a strawberry sauce, chop 100 g/3½ oz of the strawberries and mix them with 2 tablespoons of the icing sugar. Whizz in a food processor until smooth, then push through a sieve. Whip the cream with the remaining icing sugar and spread over the meringue. Drizzle over the strawberry sauce, place the strawberries on top and serve immediately.

SERVES 6–8

INGREDIENTS

85 g/3 oz
wholemeal
breadcrumbs

butter, for greasing

85 g/3 oz granulated
sugar

4 tbsp water

450 ml/16 fl oz
double cream

55 g/2 oz icing
sugar, sifted

2 tbsp dark rum

1 tsp vanilla extract

Brown Bread Ice Cream

This delicious crunchy ice cream is very simple to make and, unlike many ice creams, doesn't require frequent removal from the freezer for stirring.

METHOD

Spread the breadcrumbs on a baking tray and toast under a hot grill until golden brown. Leave to cool.

Grease a separate baking tray. Put the sugar and water into a saucepan and heat over a low heat until the sugar has dissolved Bring to the boil and bubble until the syrup is a rich caramel colour. Remove from the heat and stir in the breadcrumbs.

Turn out onto the prepared tray and leave to harden. Break the caramel into pieces and grind them using a pestle and mortar.

Whip the cream until soft peaks form, then beat in the icing sugar, rum and vanilla extract. Fold in the caramel crumbs, pou into a freezerproof container, then cover and freeze for at least 3–4 hours without stirring.

SERVES 6

INGREDIENTS

1 tbsp dried
carrageen moss
700 ml/1¼ pints
milk
200 ml/7 fl oz
double cream
2 eggs, separated
1 tbsp caster sugar
1 tsp vanilla extract
fresh berries, to
decorate (optional)

Blackberry coulis
250 g/9 oz
blackberries
100 g/3½ oz icing
sugar

Carrageen Pudding with Blackberry Coulis

Carrageen moss is a good vegetarian gelling agent and makes an excellent base for any cooked cream pudding.

METHOD

Soak the carrageen moss in hot water for 15 minutes, then drain and squeeze out any excess water. Put it into a saucepan with the milk and cream and bring to the boil over a medium heat. Reduce the heat to low and simmer for 30 minutes.

Beat the egg yolks with the sugar and vanilla extract. Pour the milk mixture through a sieve into a separate bowl, then whisk with the egg mixture until combined.

Whisk the egg whites until stiff peaks form, then fold them into the egg and milk mixture. Pour into six dariole moulds and transfer to the fridge for 3 hours, or until set.

To make the coulis, combine the blackberries with the sugar in a bowl, then purée with a hand-held blender. Press through a fine sieve into a bowl.

To serve, turn out the puddings onto small serving plates, then drizzle with the coulis. Decorate with fresh berries, if using.

SERVES 6

INGREDIENTS

500 g/1 lb 2 oz ready-made trifle sponges

150 ml/5 fl oz medium sherry

250 g/9 oz raspberry jam

600 ml/1 pint whipped cream

flaked almonds and fresh raspberries, to decorate

Creamy vanilla custard

600 ml/1 pint double cream

4 large egg yolks

1 tbsp caster sugar

1 tsp vanilla extract

Sherry Trifle

This is traditionally served at Christmas as an alternative to the heavier Christmas pudding, but it's delicious at any time of the year.

METHOD

Put the trifle sponges in the base of a large glass bowl and pour over the sherry. When it has soaked in, add the jam, spreading evenly.

To make the custard, heat the cream in a large saucepan over a medium heat until hot but not boiling. Meanwhile, whisk the egg yolks, sugar and vanilla extract together in a bowl, then gradually pour in the hot cream and whisk to combine.

Transfer to a clean saucepan and heat over a low heat, stirring constantly, until the custard has thickened. Do not allow it to come to the boil.

Pour the custard over the jam and leave to chill overnight. Just before serving, spread the whipped cream over the top and sprinkle with the flaked almonds. Decorate with raspberries.

SERVES 8–10

INGREDIENTS

4 egg yolks

75 g/2¾ oz caster sugar

200 g/7 oz mascarpone cheese

300 ml/10 fl oz double cream, whipped

100 ml/3½ fl oz brandy

450 ml/16 fl oz strong black coffee

200 g/7 oz sponge fingers

cocoa powder, for dusting

Tiramisù

The name of this Italian dessert literally means 'pick me up', which is probably the intended effect of the brandy.

METHOD

Beat the egg yolks with the sugar until pale and thick, then beat in the mascarpone cheese until smooth. Carefully fold in the cream and brandy.

Pour the coffee into a shallow dish, then dip half the sponge fingers in it, turning until they are completely soaked, but not falling apart.

Arrange the dipped sponge fingers in the base of a shallow rectangular serving dish. Spread half the mascarpone mixture over the fingers. Dip the remaining sponge fingers in the coffee and arrange them on top of the mascarpone layer, then spread or pipe the remaining mascarpone mixture on top.

Cover and chill for at least 2 hours, then dust with cocoa powder and serve.

SERVES 10

INGREDIENTS

300 ml/10 fl oz
water
55 g/2 oz caster
sugar
500 ml/16 fl oz
sparkling white wine
4 gelatine leaves
150 g/5½ oz fresh
raspberries, plus
extra to decorate
fresh mint leaves, to
decorate

Sparkling Raspberry Jellies

These individual jellies look lovely and
make a light and refreshing dessert after a
heavy meal.

METHOD

Put the water and sugar into a saucepan and heat over a low
heat until the sugar is dissolved, then increase the heat to
medium and bring to the boil. Reduce the heat and simmer for
5 minutes, then remove from the heat and set aside.

Pour the wine into a heatproof bowl, add the gelatine leaves
and leave to soak for 5 minutes. Remove the leaves, squeezing
out the liquid, and add them to the sugar syrup. Whisk to
dissolve the leaves, then add the syrup to the wine and whisk t
combine.

Leave to cool completely, then chill in the fridge for 1 hour.
Stir in the raspberries, then divide the jelly between six bowls
or glasses. Cover with clingfilm and chill for 6 hours, or until
completely set. Decorate with raspberries and mint and serve.

SERVES 6

INGREDIENTS

450 g/1 lb self-raising flour, plus extra for dusting

pinch of salt

100 g/3½ oz chilled butter, diced

85 g/3 oz caster sugar

100 ml/3½ fl oz buttermilk

1 egg, beaten, for brushing

White Buttermilk Scones

These lovely scones are perfect for a wet afternoon, with a pot of tea and lashings of butter and home-made jam.

METHOD

Preheat the oven to 220°C/425°F/Gas Mark 7. Dust a baking sheet with flour.

Put the flour, salt and butter into a bowl and rub it in with your fingertips until the mixture forms fine crumbs. Add the sugar and mix to combine.

Heat the buttermilk over a low heat until lukewarm. Gradually add to the flour mixture, cutting it in with a knife until just combined.

Turn out the dough onto a work surface lightly dusted with flour and bring it together with your hands. Press it out to a thickness of 4 cm/1½ inches, then use a 6-cm/2½-inch round biscuit cutter to cut out 12 rounds, reshaping the trimmings as necessary.

Place the scones on the prepared baking sheet, then brush with the beaten egg and bake in the preheated oven for 10–12 minutes until golden. Remove from the oven and transfer to a wire rack to cool slightly. Serve warm.

MAKES 12

INGREDIENTS

175 g/6 oz wholemeal flour, plus extra for dusting

175 g/6 oz plain flour

1 tsp bicarbonate of soda

½ tsp salt

55 g/2 oz butter

1 tbsp soft light brown sugar

200 ml/7 fl oz buttermilk

1 egg, beaten, for glazing

Wholemeal Scones

You could add a little chopped thyme and about 55 g/2 oz grated Cheddar cheese to the dough for a savoury treat.

METHOD

Preheat the oven to 200°C/400°F/Gas Mark 6. Dust a baking sheet with flour.

Put the wholemeal flour, plain flour, salt and bicarbonate of soda into a bowl and mix to combine. Add the butter and rub it in with your fingertips until the mixture forms fine crumbs. Add the sugar and mix to combine.

Stir in enough buttermilk to make a soft dough. Turn out onto a work surface lightly dusted with flour and knead for about 10 seconds.

Press out the dough to a thickness of 4 cm/1½ inches, then use a 6-cm/2½-inch round biscuit cutter to cut out 8–10 rounds, reshaping the trimmings as necessary.

Place the scones on the prepared baking sheet, then brush with the beaten egg and bake in the preheated oven for 15 minutes, or until risen and golden. Transfer to a wire rack to cool slightly. Serve warm.

MAKES 8-10

INGREDIENTS

675 g/1 lb 8 oz
wholemeal flour

450 g/1 lb strong
white flour, plus
extra for dusting

2 tsp bicarbonate
of soda

2 tsp salt

750 ml/1½ pints
buttermilk, plus extra
if needed

Brown Soda Bread

This is a wholemeal alternative to white soda bread. Wholemeal flour on its own would make too dense a loaf, so white flour is always added to the mixture.

METHOD

Preheat the oven to 230°C/450°F/Gas Mark 8. Dust a large baking sheet with flour.

Mix the dry ingredients together in a large mixing bowl, then make a well in the centre and gradually add the buttermilk, drawing in the dry ingredients from the side of the bowl. Mix until a soft dough forms, adding more buttermilk if necessary. The dough should not be too moist.

Turn out the dough onto a work surface lightly dusted with flour, then divide into two pieces and shape both pieces into a round about 5 cm/2 inches high. Place on the prepared baking sheet and use a floured knife to cut a deep cross in each loaf.

Bake in the preheated oven for 15–20 minutes, then reduce the oven temperature to 200°C/400°F/Gas Mark 6 and bake for a further 20–25 minutes until the loaves sound hollow when tapped on the base. Transfer to a wire rack and leave to cool.

MAKES 2 LOAVES

INGREDIENTS

vegetable oil, for
greasing
1.3 kg/3 lb
wholemeal flour
500 ml/18 fl oz
water
500 ml/18 fl oz milk
1 tbsp soft light
brown sugar
55 g/2 oz fresh
yeast
2 tsp salt
milk, for brushing

Brown Bread

This nutty yeast bread has a slightly sweet
flavour. It's well worth taking the time
needed to prepare it with fresh yeast.

METHOD

Grease two 900-g/2-lb loaf tins and the inside of two large
polythene bags.

Put half the flour into a large mixing bowl. Mix the milk and
water together in a jug, then add the sugar and yeast. Add to the
flour and beat well. Cover the bowl with a damp tea towel and
leave to stand for 10–15 minutes until the mixture is frothy.

Add the remaining flour and the salt and mix to a soft dough.
Knead for 10 minutes.

Divide the dough into two pieces and place a piece in each
of the prepared tins. Put the tins into the prepared bags and
leave to stand until the dough has risen to the top of the tins.
Meanwhile, preheat the oven to 230°C/450°F/Gas Mark 8.

Brush the tops of the loaves with milk and bake in the
preheated oven for 30–40 minutes until risen and golden
brown and they sound hollow when tapped on the base. Leave
to cool in the tins for 10 minutes, then transfer to a wire rack
and leave to cool completely.

MAKES 2 LOAVES

INGREDIENTS

225 g/8 oz porridge oats, plus extra for dusting

60 g/2¼ oz wholemeal flour, plus extra for dusting

½ tsp bicarbonate of soda

1 tsp salt

½ tsp sugar

4–5 tbsp hot water

Crunchy Savoury Oatcakes

These are very quick and easy to prepare and are delicious with any kind of cheese or smoked fish.

METHOD

Preheat the oven to 190°C/375°F/Gas Mark 5.

Put the oats, flour, bicarbonate of soda, salt and sugar into a bowl and mix to combine. Add the butter and rub it in until the mixture has the consistency of coarse breadcrumbs.

Gradually add the water and mix until the dough is thick but not sticky.

Roll out the dough on a work surface lightly dusted with a mixture of oats and flour, to a thickness of 5 mm/¼ inch. Cut out 12 rounds with a fluted biscuit cutter and place on a baking tray.

Bake in the preheated oven for 20–30 minutes, until golden. Leave to cool on the tray until firm, then transfer to a wire rack to cool completely. Store in an airtight container until needed.

SERVES 12

INGREDIENTS

115 g/4 oz butter, softened

115 g/4 oz mature Cheddar cheese, grated

1 tsp chopped fresh thyme

½ tsp salt

½ tsp freshly ground black pepper

175 g/6 oz plain flour, plus extra for dusting

finely snipped chives and chive blossoms, to garnish

soft cheese, to serve

Cheese & Herb Crackers

A delicious addition to the cheeseboard, these crisp crackers go particularly well with mild soft cheeses.

METHOD

Cream the butter for 1 minute, then add the cheese, thyme, salt and pepper and mix to combine. Add the flour and combine for about 1 minute until the mixture is crumbly.

Turn out the dough onto a work surface lightly dusted with flour and press into a ball. Roll the ball into a 23-cm/9-inch log. Wrap in clingfilm and chill for at least 30 minutes.

Meanwhile, preheat the oven to 180°C/350°F/Gas Mark 4. Line a baking tray with baking paper. Cut the log into 24 rounds and place them on the prepared tray.

Bake in the preheated oven for 22 minutes until golden brown, turning the tin halfway through cooking.

Leave the crackers to cool on the tray for 5 minutes, then transfer to a wire rack and leave to cool completely.

Serve with the cheese of your choice, garnished with chives.

MAKES 24

INGREDIENTS

500 g/1 lb 2 oz
Bramley apples,
peeled, cored and
cut into chunks

2 tbsp soft light
brown sugar

250 g/9 oz plain
flour, plus extra if
needed

½ tsp baking powder

100 g/3½ oz chilled
butter, plus extra for
greasing

100 g/3½ oz caster
sugar

1 large egg, beaten

100 ml/3½ fl oz
milk

Irish Apple Cake

This cake is a cross between an apple tart
and an apple pie. The texture of the pastry
– a bit like a soft shortbread – is key.

METHOD

Preheat the oven to 180°C/350°F/Gas Mark 4. Grease a
20-cm/8-inch round loose-based cake tin and line the base
with baking paper.

Toss the apples with the brown sugar. Sift the flour and baking
powder together into a bowl and rub in the butter until fine
crumbs form.

Add the caster sugar to the butter mixture, mixing it in with a
blunt knife, then add the egg. Very gradually add the milk until
a soft dough forms. Add more flour if the dough becomes too
wet to handle.

Spread half the dough in the base of the prepared tin. Tip
in the apples, then place the remaining dough on top. Bake
in the preheated oven for 40 minutes, or until the dough is
golden and the apples are tender. Leave to cool in the tin for
about 10 minutes, then turn out and serve.

SERVES 8

INGREDIENTS

450 g/1 lb plain flour

½ tsp freshly grated nutmeg

pinch of salt

15 g/½ oz fresh yeast

55 g/2 oz soft light brown sugar

300 ml/10 fl oz lukewarm milk

2 eggs, beaten

55 g/2 oz butter, plus extra for greasing

115 g/4 oz mixed peel

225 g/8 oz currants

225 g/8 oz raisins

1 egg yolk, beaten, for glazing

Brack

Made with yeast, this traditional Halloween treat is a sweet bread rather than a cake.

METHOD

Grease a 20-cm/8-inch round cake tin. Sift the flour, nutmeg and salt into a large mixing bowl.

In a separate bowl, blend the yeast with 1 teaspoon of the sugar and a little of the milk until it froths.

Add the remaining sugar to the flour mixture. Add the remaining milk to the yeast mixture, then add to the flour along with the eggs and butter. Mix with a wooden spoon for about 10 minutes until stiff.

Fold in the mixed peel, currants and raisins, then transfer the mixture to the prepared tin. Cover with a damp tea towel and leave to rise for about 1 hour until doubled in size.

Meanwhile, preheat the oven to 200°C/400°F/Gas Mark 6. Bake the brack in the preheated oven for 1 hour, then glaze with the beaten egg yolk and bake for a further 5 minutes. Leave to cool in the tin for 10 minutes, then turn out onto a wire rack and leave to cool completely.

SERVES 10-12

INGREDIENTS

125 ml/4 fl oz hot strong black coffee
1 tsp soft light brown sugar
1 measure whiskey
4 tbsp double cream
chocolate nibs and marshmallows, to decorate (optional)

Irish Coffee

This deliciously creamy and alcoholic coffee drink is a traditional way to round off a celebratory meal.

METHOD

Put a teaspoon in a wine glass and pour in the coffee.

Add the sugar and stir to dissolve, then add the whiskey and stir.

Very slowly pour the cream into the glass over the back of the spoon. Decorate with chocolate nibs and marshmallows, if using.

SERVES 1

INGREDIENTS

1 measure Irish whiskey

2 tsp soft light brown sugar

slice of lemon or orange

5 cloves

1 cinnamon stick

Hot Whiskey

A really good way to warm up after a brisk walk on a cold Sunday afternoon!

METHOD

Heat a glass using hot water and place a teaspoon in it.

Add the whiskey, sugar, lemon, cloves and cinnamon stick, then top up with boiling water.

Stir gently until the sugar is dissolved, then serve immediately.

SERVES 1

The Story of Irish Whiskey

Whiskey (from the Irish *uisce beatha*, meaning water of life) was first distilled in Ireland by monks returning from continental Europe with perfume-distilling skills. They adapted these to the production of a spirit for the consumption of the monks, and soon the science of distilling had spread outside the confines of the monastic walls. In 1608 Bushmills in Northern Ireland became the first licensed distillery in the world when King James I granted it a royal charter.

Whiskey became very popular in Ireland and Britain in the 18th and 19th centuries, with a huge number of illegal distilleries contributing to the flourishing trade in whiskey. In 1820 there were only 20 legal distilleries – the remaining 800 were unlicensed.

Several things led to an enormous downturn in the fortunes of the Irish whiskey industry. Alcohol abuse was a huge problem, and in 1838 Father Theobald Mathew founded the Total Abstinence Association in an effort to combat this. The declining market for whiskey resulted in the closure of many of the smaller distilleries. Their loss was the gain of the larger concerns, including those run by the Power and Jameson families of Dublin.

Despite the weakness of the Irish market, by 1900 Irish whiskey was the most popular spirit in Britain and was being exported in large quantities to the US. However, the introduction of prohibition there in 1920 destroyed that market and the growing popularity of Scotch blended whisky in Britain eroded Irish sales there. Blended whiskies could be produced far more quickly than the Irish single malts, so they were cheaper and more readily available. By 1960, the exportation of Irish whiskey had ground to a halt and sales were also dwindling in Ireland.

However, its popularity revived and today there is a solid home market, with good sales in continental Europe and a developing market in China and Russia. If you'd like to find out more about the Irish whiskey story, there are excellent visitor centres at the Old Jameson Distillery in Dublin, and at the Tullamore D.E.W. Distillery in Tullamore.

INGREDIENTS

2 measures ruby port
4 cloves
1 lemon slice
sugar, to taste

Hot Port

Hot port is the quintessential pub drink on a cold winter's afternoon. One is probably quite enough!

METHOD

Pour the port into a glass, add the cloves and lemon slice and top up with hot water, adding a little sugar if liked.

SERVES 1

INGREDIENTS

600 ml/1 pint
Guinness
600 ml/1 pint
chilled Champagne

Black Velvet

An unlikely combination, this Guinness
and Champagne cocktail really works. You
could make it with any sparkling wine.

METHOD

Half-fill a glass of your choice with Guinness, then very slowly fill
it to the top with Champagne over the back of a spoon into it.

Serve immediately.

SERVES 1

INGREDIENTS

1 shot blackcurrant cordial

600 ml/1 pint Guinness

Guinness & Black

Blackcurrant cordial transforms a pint of the black stuff into something that tastes a bit like a Black Forest gâteau. It may not be for Guinness purists, but it's delicious, all the same.

METHOD

Pour the cordial into a pint glass, then pour in the Guinness in the usual way and serve.

SERVES 1

INGREDIENTS

600 m l/1 pint
Guinness
600 ml/1 pint cider

Black Adder

Otherwise known as a Poor Man's Black
Velvet, this is made with cider.

METHOD

Half-fill a glass of your choice with Guinness, then very slowly
fill it up to the top with cider over the back of a spoon to fill
each glass.

Serve immediately.

SERVES 1

INGREDIENTS

125 ml/4 fl oz
whiskey
500 ml/18 fl oz milk
1 tbsp clear honey
½ tsp ground ginger
½ tsp freshly grated
nutmeg

Scailtín

This milk punch tastes almost too
wholesome to be alcoholic – good for
lining the stomach!

METHOD

Heat the whiskey and milk in a small saucepan over a low heat
until warm, then stir in the honey and ginger.

Continue to heat, whisking constantly, but do not allow the
mixture to come to the boil.

Pour into two mugs, sprinkle with nutmeg and serve
immediately.

SERVES 2

For permission to reproduce copyright photographs, the publisher gratefully acknowledges the following:

p1 Michael Diggin
p2 Michael Diggin
p7 iPics
p10 Michael Diggin
p13 Shutterstock/Magdanatka
p15 Shutterstock/Gorenkova Evgenija
p17 Shutterstock/Ezume Images
p19 Shutterstock/Svetlana Foote
p21 Shutterstock/Anna Pustynnikova
p23 Shutterstock/Magdanatka
p25 Shutterstock/Bartosz Luczak
p27 Shutterstock/Rihardzz
p29 Shutterstock/Fanfo
p31 Shutterstock/Fanfo
p33 Ben Potter
p35 Shutterstock/Omar Challard
p37 Shutterstock/Monkey Business
p39 Shutterstock/Antonio Danna
p41 Shutterstock/Sarsmis
p43 Shutterstock/Warren Price Photography
p45 Shutterstock/Lisovskaya Natalia
p47 Shutterstock/Douglas Freer
p49 Shutterstock/Salvomassara
p51 Ben Potter
p53 Ben Potter
p55 Ben Potter
p57 Ben Potter
p59 Ben Potter
p61 Ben Potter
p63 Shutterstock/Nadiia Diachenko
p65 Ben Potter

p67 Shutterstock/Mama Mia
p69 Ben Potter
p71 Shutterstock/CatchaSnap
p73 Shutterstock/Timolina
p75 Ben Potter
p76–77 Michael Diggin
p79 Ben Potter
p81 Shutterstock/Bonchan
p83 Ben Potter
p85 Michael Diggin
p87 Shutterstock/Geshas
p89 Shutterstock/Z. Kruger
p91 Ben Potter
p93 Shutterstock/Joe Gough
p95 Shutterstock/Mama Mia
p97 Shutterstock/Nataliia Doroshenko
p99 Ben Potter/Amallia Eka
p101 Shutterstock/Taiftin
p103 Shutterstock/Travellight
p105 Shutterstock/Riggsby
p107 Shutterstock/Stella Grzela
p109 Shutterstock/Vkuslandia
p111 Shutterstock/Farbled
p113 Shutterstock/Joshua Resnick
p115 Shutterstock/Prapass
p117 Shutterstock/Magdanatka
p119 Ben Potter
p121 Shutterstock/Olaf Speier
p123 Shutterstock/Inkru
p125 Ben Potter
p127 Ben Potter
p129 Shutterstock/Inkru
p131 Ben Potter
p133 Shutterstock/Chris Green
p134–135 Shutterstock/Littleny

p137 Ben Potter
p139 Ben Potter
p141 Ben Potter
p143 Ben Potter
p145 Shutterstock/Joerg Beuge
p147 Shutterstock/JeniFoto
p149 Shutterstock/Neil Langan
p151 Shutterstock/Fanfo
p153 Ben Potter
p155 Shutterstock/Africa Studio
p157 Shutterstock/Stephen Gibson
p159 Shutterstock/Brent Hofacker
p161 Shutterstock/Vankad
p163 Shutterstock/Robyn Mackenzie
p165 Ben Potter
p167 Shutterstock/Z. Kruger
p169 Shutterstock/Stuart Monk
p171 Shutterstock/Robin Stewart
p173 Ben Potter
p175 Shutterstock/A. Zhuravleva
p177 Ben Potter
p179 Ben Potter
p180–181 Shutterstock/Litteny
p183 Shutterstock/Lesya Dolyuk
p185 Shutterstock/Nataliya Arzamasova
p187 Shutterstock/Qanat Studio
p189 Shutterstock/Yulia Davidovich
p191 Ben Potter
p193 Ben Potter
p195 Shutterstock/Napapat Kulsomboon

p197 Shutterstock/Baboyan Flora
p199 Ben Potter
p201 Shutterstock/Monkey Business Images
p203 Shutterstock/Douglas Freer
p205 Shutterstock/Farbled
p207 Shutterstock/Elena Shashkina
p209 Ben Potter
p211 Shutterstock/Kuvona
p213 Ben Potter
p215 Shutterstock/Nadki
p217 Shutterstock/Charles Knox
p218–219 Micheal Diggin
p221 Shutterstock/Floral
p223 Shutterstock/Jim Bowie
p225 Shutterstock/Leigh Boardman
p227 Shutterstock/Nata-Lia
p229 Shutterstock/Space Monkey Pics
p231 Ben Potter
p233 Shutterstock/Kati Molin
p235 Shutterstock/M. Shev
p237 Ben Potter
p238–239 Micheal Diggin
p241 Shutterstock/Eduard Zhukov
p243 Shutterstock/Liv Friis-larsen
p245 Shutterstock/Drserg
p247 Ben Potter
p249 Ben Potter
p251 Shutterstock/Oislavicek
p253 Ben Potter
p255 Shutterstock/Africa Studio